SOCIAL CHANGE & Religious Faith

CYNTHIA HAWKINSON
ALDEN L. WEIGHT

www.kendallhunt.com
Send all inquiries to:
4050 Westmark Drive
Dubuque, IA 52004-1840

TABLE OF CONTENTS

ACKNOWLEDGEMENTS

The authors would like to thank our families and friends

who have patiently encouraged our endless discussions

of social change and religious faith as well as supported us in countless ways:

John, Ben, Aubrey, Liam, Sam, Jacob, Amber,

Steph, Raquelle, Josh, Mario, Leslie, Marie, Christie, James, and Derek.

Thanks as well to our interviewees Kim and Liz for their willingness

to participate in this project with us.

We would also like to thank our colleagues Nick Alozie and Mark Simpson

for providing helpful advice and feedback throughout this project.

PREFACE

Notes from the Authors

Please note that these conversations occur at several points throughout the book and represent the authors' personal viewpoints, experiences, and conclusions. The views we express in these conversations are our own as private citizens and are not meant to represent the perspectives or policies of any other person, social group, or institution, including those of the religious organizations we attend or of our employer, Arizona State University.

Cynthia: Once again, it was time to order a textbook for the university course that I teach about social change. I read through many chapters of several textbooks, and the Table of Contents and summaries of many more, but was frustrated to realize that two items were consistently missing:

1. a concise, comprehensive definition of "social change," and

2. a thorough discussion of religion as a motivator (trigger, driver, or force) of social change within the hearts and minds of the change agents (individual person, groups of people, or organizations).

Quite a few textbooks and journal articles alike merely mention religion as a contributor to or motivator of social change (University of Minnesota Libraries 2010[1], for instance), but there aren't many in-depth discussions.

Alden: Meanwhile, in the office next door, I was grading papers from my sociology of religion students. Many were interested in religion in the abstract, and they appreciated the historical role of religion in world history—the actions of Pope Alexander VI leading to the Treaty of Tordesillas played a seminal role in shaping the Western Hemisphere in the late fifteenth century, after all. Early American history had religion scattered throughout its social change, from the Separatists

(Continued)

---

[1] The University of Minnesota Libraries host a series of university-published texts, including an introductory sociology textbook. Its brief admission that religion may contribute to social change is found in its Chapter 17. See https://open.lib.umn.edu/sociology/chapter/17-3-sociological-perspectives-on-religion/. This appears to be the typical approach in the existing literature. More in-depth or extensive discussions of religion as a motivator of social change are likewise rare.

on the Mayflower to the deism of the Founding Fathers. From the pragmatism of Brigham Young to the spiritualism of Abraham Lincoln, religion has been a persistent theme throughout American history. Even as recently as Martin Luther King Jr. and Mother Teresa, students clearly understood religion had been important in historic social change.

Still, quite a few students wondered about the relevance of religion in modern life—that is, whether religion is *still* important in history and to current difference-makers—and they wondered *why* religion had been important. And so, Cynthia and I struck up a conversation about religion's role in social change.

Cynthia: It is hard for me to imagine that we can study anything in depth without first developing a clear and detailed definition of what we are studying. Of course, it is possible that I happened to simply not stumble across the textbooks with such a definition, but nonetheless, I was surprised with my findings. Most textbooks took a limited approach, particularly emphasizing the sociological aspects of social change.

And, yes, a few textbooks do provide a discussion of religion as a driver of social change, but typically such discussions were focused on radical terrorists that use religion as a justification for violence. However, it appears that religious or ideological difference are likely not the root cause of violence, but instead, poverty or lack of resources are more likely the root cause. I was frustrated in not finding a much more robust discussion of religious belief as a motivator of social change.

Alden: As readers of this book will see, I have long been fascinated by Edward Bailey's (2011) idea of implicit religion — simply explained, the idea that religion is a manifestation of a deeper collective impulse involving patterns and ideas greater than ourselves that exist in a wide variety of social settings. Émile Durkheim's (2008) famous conclusion that religion is society echoes this. So we see ideas and behavior that very much resemble religion and religious behavior in other areas of human behavior, notably sports, politics, the arts, journalism, and even the sciences. Even social activists who have shunned religion as misleading or potentially harmful nonsense have worked out of an interest of serving a cause greater than themselves—reaching out to their fellow humans in order to make their world better. This impulse needed to be explained.

Even more than that, I was just as dissatisfied as Cynthia with finding only shallow and ultimately misleading coverage of religion as a motivator of social change, mentioned often only in the context of atrocity or cruelty. To cite only one example, there is much more—MUCH more!—to the story of religion and social change than Islamic terrorism. Improperly focusing on this facet not only misrepresents Islam in the manner the vast majority of Muslims practice it, but falsely suggests that extremism and terrorism are only an Islamic issue. In fact, extremists and terrorists exist in virtually *every* major world religion, even if the activities of Buddhist, Christian, or Sikh terrorists get relatively little press by comparison.

(Continued)

We fully recognize that various negative aspects of religion are part of the issue and necessary to consider. We have acknowledged relevant downsides as we have felt appropriate. However, neither of us are experts in deviance, terrorism, cult behavior, or other distinct negatives of religious practice. We also felt that undue focus on the proverbial dark side of religious belief and behavior would shut out the tremendous good that many other religious people have tried to accomplish over the centuries. For these reasons, it seemed more productive to focus on the positive side of social change and examine how religion has contributed to change for the better—how, to paraphrase the well-known words attributed to Mahatma Gandhi (though as discussed at the end of our book, it's been disputed that he actually said this), religion has inspired people to "be the change they wish to see in the world."

Cynthia: After a great deal of thought, I decided that a short book on religious faith as a motivator of social change was in order, and I asked Alden to join me in this adventure.

Alden: I agreed. And so, we got to work. As the idea for the book evolved, we also decided it would be useful to include some of our conclusions about why religion seems to motivate individuals to accomplish social change. So throughout the text, we have made notes in the interest of explaining our observations—thereby contributing some of the initial bricks towards building a theory of religion and social change.

© John Gomez/Shutterstock.com

For the readers' interest and so that we are transparent with our readers, we want to acknowledge our personal religious backgrounds. I am an active member of The Church of Jesus Christ of Latter-day Saints, while Cynthia is an active member of a community Protestant Christian church. Our faith experiences have given us insight into the motivating power of religion to drive social change

An unidentified clergyman protests for climate change at The Time is Now rally near Parliment in London on June 26, 2019.

and helped us meet people who apply their religion in the social change they actively strive to accomplish. Later in the book, readers will meet some of these people whose faith matters so much to them that it inspires them to try to change the world—or at least the world around them.

As Cynthia and I continue our conversation, which has produced this book, we hope readers see and understand that religion can and does still play a key role in social change for many people in the world around us—even if that religion is, in Bailey's terms, implicit religion. We hope all who read this book will find insight and understanding, and possibly, motivation to make social change.

CHAPTER 1

DEFINING "SOCIAL CHANGE"

Never doubt that a small group of thoughtful, committed citizens can change the world; indeed, it's the only thing that ever has.

—Quote frequently attributed to Margaret Mead[1]

© arindambanerjee/Shutterstock.com

"Keep your coins, I want change!" is
a powerful concept for social change.

Let's start our discussion of social change and religious faith by piecing together a clear, concise working definition of "social change." As we proceed in the next few chapters, and throughout the rest of the book, we will build onto this definition to explain how religion motivates social change.

---

[1] There is some debate about whether Margaret Mead actually made this statement, though the quote, along with others, can be found at https://www.brainyquote.com/quotes/margaret_mead_100502.

Traditionally, sociologists have followed three separate theories when defining social change, specifically: 1) evolutionary, 2) conflict, and 3) functionalist theory. The **evolutionary perspective** defines social change through the lens of a complex, evolving social system, similar to a living organism that is forever changing through time. This is a very common perspective amongst sociologists, as shown by these recently published definitions:

"Social change is the way in which culture, interaction, and innovation change social institutions over time" (Carl 2010).

"The dynamic forces that have shaped our way of life, ranging from innovations in technology to the growth of bureaucracy and the expansion of cities. These are all dimensions of social change, the transformation of culture and social institutions over time. The process of social change has four major characteristics: 1) social change happens all the time; 2) social change is sometimes intentional but often it is unplanned; 3) social change is controversial; and 4) some changes matter more than others" (Macionis 2014).

"Social change can be defined as the transformation over time of the institutions and culture of society. [It is the] alteration in basic structures of a social group or society. Social change is an ever-present phenomenon in social life" (Giddens 2017).

Social change occurs as "the culture of a society is constantly evolving to fit new situations" (Hunt 2011).

Social change is the "significant alteration over time in behavior patterns and culture, including norms and values. Social change can occur so slowly as to be almost undetectable to those it affects, but it can also happen with breathtaking rapidity" (Witt 2009).

Conflict theory defines social change through the perspective of competition, conflicting interests, uneasy tension (seen in subtle ways but sometimes escalating to protests, as we know all too well, and on particularly intense occasions, all-out war), and the resolution of the conflict. Competition may occur for almost any limited resource, including natural or human resources, but also political or social power.

"Change is the preeminent characteristic of modern human societies, whether it occurs in personal relations, cultural norms and values, systems of stratification or institutions… Sociologists who focus on change tell us that institutional transformations are more likely to be caused over time by a variety of social forces, including environmental and population pressures, cultural innovation, and technological and cultural diffusion" (Newman 2011).

"For most people, what they take to be social change feels very personal and local… Personal experiences, however, are a part of something bigger than themselves, something very social. Social change can be thought of as the sum total of many people's personal experiences in social context undergoing change… Relationships, group norms, beliefs, technologies, and material objects extend beyond the individual. The idea that social change is an individual experience differing from what others—at an earlier time—have experienced is incomplete if it does not examine the social processes, powerful forces, and networks of relationships surrounding the experiences" (Massey 2016).

Finally, the **functionalist perspective** defines social change through the changing needs of a society. If any of the various interconnected, interdependent parts of the social system stops serving a functional need within the production of a stable social structure, it is removed from the system.

"Sociologists define social change as the alteration, modification, or transformation of public policy, culture, or social institutions over time. Social change is usually brought about by collective behavior and social movements" (Kendall 2011).

"Sociology is largely the study of social change, change in the structure of society and in its institutions… Sociologists believe that social systems change when powerful internal or external forces influence them such that the previous social order can no longer be maintained. However, societies are complex, inter-dependent systems of values, norms, and institutions; they are often amazingly resistant to change and rarely transformed by the ideas or behaviors of a single person. When a major change does occur, however, it influences the entire society; each social institution must adapt to the new order" (Basirico 2009).

Given the definitions above and a bit of our own insight, our working definition of "social change" is:

Social change is a significant alteration of culture, demography, economic pursuits, governmental/political activity, science/technology, and/or social institutions within a society over time.

Students in Australia advocate for climate change in March 2019.

© Holli/Shutterstock.com

With our definition, keep in mind the following three observations:

1. If social change is as Massey (2016) states, "the sum total of many people's personal experiences," then **social change is not just one person's or a few people's personal experiences** (such as a family's move from one city to another), **and also not a common life event** (such as getting married). Moving from one place to another is a personal experience and not social change, unless the move is part of an overall change of migration within a society—a demographic change. Getting married is a personal experience and not social change, unless the laws of marriage within a society have changed allowing marriages that were previously not allowed, such as same-sex marriages or multi-racial marriages—a social institution and governmental change.

2. **Each incident of social change is unique and moves at its own pace**. There are so many variables involved in social change that it is quite difficult to predict which change will be pushed forward by which change agents, the speed of the social change, and which change will be accepted or rejected in a somewhat permanent manner by any particular society. It is important to note that the speed at which social change occurs varies with each incident and within each society. As Witt (2009) tells us, "Social change can occur so slowly as to be almost undetectable to those it affects, but it can also happen with breathtaking rapidity."

3. **Not all social change is seen as good or desirable**. In fact, an entire society rarely accepts a social change when it first comes to light. Basirico (2009) stated that societies "are often amazingly resistant to change." There are almost always a few vocal individuals or large groups of people who lag behind or who adamantly, and sometimes forcefully, resist change. This resistance slows the change process. This resistance may stop the change process or even cause a reversal back to a previous pattern within the society. Some social change movements specifically demand change back to a preferred (sometimes idealized) point in time, back to "the good ole days."

For example, the Right-to-Life movement (https://www.nrlc.org/), also known as the pro-life movement, in the United States continues to push for the overturning of the 1973 *Roe v. Wade* Supreme Court decision, which established a woman's legal right to an abortion in all fifty states (https://www.history.com/topics/womens-rights/roe-v-wade and https://www.oah.org/tah/issues/2016/november/abolishing-abortion-the-history-of-the-pro-life-movement-in-america/).

Some social change is not only undesirable, but ends up producing disastrous consequences, possibly even triggering war between societies. For example: Nazi Germany's assimilation of neighboring European countries prior to World War II and the subsequent ethnic cleansing (the imprisonment and murder of millions of Jewish people) was most definitely social change for the worse and launched warfare that involved many countries across the globe (https://www.history.com/topics/world-war-ii/the-holocaust and https://guides.lib.jjay.cuny.edu/c.php?g=288386&p=1922582).

Alden: I know that you have been very involved in social change. What made you who you are, a social activist?

Cynthia: Having grown up in the 1960s and '70s, I saw huge social change in America during my childhood. In the '60s, though I was very young, I remember seeing the news on our black-and-white TV documenting the Detroit race riots, the hippie movement, the race to put a man on the moon, and the Vietnam War with its anti-war movement. In the '70s as an older child and teenager, I remember crying during nuclear bomb drills at school (Cold War era), and being oddly hypnotized by the news coverage of the Nixon impeachment proceedings and the evacuation of Saigon. I remember desperately wanting to join the Sierra Club and the Cousteau Society, but feeling very frustrated because I did not have the money to do so.

These things impacted me deeply, thus laying the groundwork for my own participation in social change.

Alden: Do you remember much about the Civil Rights Movement?

Cynthia: I was too young to remember Dr. King and his death. But I do remember that there was a white Klan cross sitting high on the hill above my town as a warning to those who lived in the town across the river. There was also a sign on the bridge that connected the two towns that said, "No Coloreds After Dark." My high school football and basketball teams only played their high school teams during the daytime. My classmates and I were painfully aware of the unfair segregation of the two towns.

Alden: What about your college years? Isn't that when most people become active in social movements?

Cynthia: Yes, many people become involved in social movements during their college years, but not me. I was still trying to understand the world around me and how I fit into that world. My father had always told me that I could be anything I wanted to be, but...

My college freshman year, I enrolled in the mechanical engineering curriculum at my state university. My freshman Calculus for Engineers class had 300+ students in it, but only two were female—myself and my high school friend. It was more than just a bit uncomfortable to have the entire class go silent, turn, and stare at me whenever I entered a classroom. But it was more uncomfortable to have my male classmates refuse to be my lab, study, and project partners. Of course, that all changed when it became evident by the end of the school year that I was one of the top students. But somehow, I was made even more uncomfortable by their new-found attention. For good or for bad, I chose to not stay in engineering. I didn't want to be uncomfortable with my colleagues for the rest of my life.

Mind you, that was the early 1980s, and I certainly was not the only one who felt the sting of prejudice and rejection just because of my gender. Fortunately, social change has occurred, and girls nowadays have much more acceptance in STEM studies.

Alden: Wow, it's sad that you had to experience that! Tell me about the areas of social change you have been involved in since your college years.

(Continued)

Cynthia: It would probably be easier to list those areas that I haven't been involved in, but maybe most notably, I have worked in the area of human trafficking. I can't tell you exactly why this specific area has hit my heart so deeply other than to say that I am simply horrified at the thought that people are willing to enslave other people. Human traffickers are, in my mind, stealing the life and liberty of another person and that just simply cannot be allowed! I cannot turn a blind eye or keep my mouth shut in the face of such injustice. Some things are just simply innately wrong!

Alden: Okay, I know you have a strong sense of religious faith. How does your faith play into your desire to make social change, including fighting human trafficking?

Cynthia: I am a Christian, which means that I see the Bible as truth and as instructions from God to make changes within me.

Micah 6:8 (NIV) says, *"He has shown you, O mortal, what is good. And what does the Lord require of you? To act justly and to love mercy and to walk humbly with your God."*

In other words, I believe that God wants me to be humble, show mercy, and act justly. This is the simple yet difficult list in which I attempt to live by, including pursuing social justice.

* The views we express in these conversations are our own as private citizens and are not meant to represent the perspectives or policies of any other person, social group, or institution, including those of the religious organizations we attend or of our employer.

It's also important to recognize that social change, in line with the observation frequently attributed to Margaret Mead, is a collective activity, though particularly influential individuals (the "who") frequently "lead out" or set the tone. Leaders direct the events, but it takes a group of people to follow them and bring about change. The purposeful events and activities that lead to social change (the "how" of social change) are relatively well-studied phenomena, including:

- marches/rallies/protests; for example: The March on Washington (https://kinginstitute.stanford.edu/encyclopedia/march-washington-jobs-and-freedom),

© Everett Collection/Shutterstock.com

The 1963 March on Washington included more than 200,000 people marching and gathering on the US Capitol Mall in support of civil rights, specifically jobs and freedom.

- sit-ins/dine-ins; for example: The Greensboro Sit-In (https://www.smithsonianmag.com/smithsonian-institution/lessons-worth-learning-moment-greensboro-four-sat-down-lunch-counter-180974087/)

- petitions; for example: The Petition for Women's Suffrage (https://history.house.gov/Records-and-Research/Listing/pm_012/),

- social media postings; for example: #MeToo (https://metoomvmt.org/),

- town hall meetings; for example: presidential candidate roundtable discussions with the voting public,

- fundraising; for example: ALS Ice Bucket Challenge (http://www.alsa.org/news/media/press-releases/Ice-Bucket-Challenge-dramatically-accelerated-the-fight-against-ALS.html),

- elections, including state-wide referendums; for example: California's 2012 Proposition 35, which imposed higher criminal penalties for human trafficking (https://vig.cdn.sos.ca.gov/2012/general/pdf/35-title-summ-analysis.pdf),

- court rulings; for example: the 2019 Supreme Court ruling in *Carpenter v. United States* which requires the government to acquire a search warrant before accessing a person's cellphone location data (https://www.aclu.org/blog/privacy-technology/location-tracking/supreme-courts-most-consequential-ruling-privacy-digital), and

- rioting; for example: The Watts Riots (http://crdl.usg.edu/events/watts_riots/?Welcome&Welcome).

Much less explored territory includes the "who" and the "why" of social change. Does the "why" select the "who" (i.e., the individual who is willing to step out of the crowd and voice the need for change)? As we will show in the following chapters, this seems to be a reasonable conclusion. Making social change is difficult and sometimes dangerous work, and therefore not many people choose to take the risk of being a visible agent of change. Why did Martin Luther King Jr., Gandhi, or Mother Theresa take the necessary action to make significant social change? In each case, these individuals held tightly to a religious faith. Is this a coincidence? We don't think so. In fact, we see religious faith as a major motivating factor (the "why") for each of these well-known agents of social change (the "who").

In Chapters 3 and 4, we will define "religious faith" and discuss the religious landscape. In Chapters 5, 6, and 7, we will examine religious faith as a motivator of social change for organizations, groups, and individuals. Chapters 8 and 9 provide case study examples of modern individuals who are making social change and are motivated by their religious faith, concluding with a discussion of religion as a motivator of social change in Chapter 10. But first, we will discuss the wide range of possible motivators of social change—also known as the "why" of social change—in Chapter 2.

Alden: So Cynthia, have you participated in social change activities and events?

Cynthia: Well, not rioting! But yes, I have signed petitions, called and sent e-mails to my representatives, spoken at town hall meetings, organized fundraising events, voted for/against candidates and propositions, attended legislative committee meetings, donated time and money, participated in postcard mailing campaigns, marched in protests, researched issues, made presentations and served as a discussion panelist, organized conferences, boycotted companies (using my consumer dollar to send a strong message), and worked with lawmakers to formulate new legislation and policy.

Alden: So, what insights would you like to share with others who also want to participate in social change?

Cynthia: Some changes are made quickly and easily, but most social change takes hard work and patience. It can be very frustrating, but keep in my mind, social justice is worth the effort!

In the years that I have been active in social change, I have never been arrested, taken to court, physically injured, or threatened by activists working on the other side of an issue. If you choose to work for social change, please remember five things:

1. Stay calm and be patient (this may take a while),

2. Respect others who may have a different opinion than yours,

3. Do your research so you are truly informed on both sides of the issue,

4. Leave before dark (never protest after nightfall), and

5. Do whatever law enforcement requests, including applying for permits and filing for non-profit organization status.

* The views we express in these conversations are our own as private citizens and are not meant to represent the perspectives or policies of any other person, social group, or institution, including those of the religious organizations we attend or of our employer.

CHAPTER 2

MOTIVATORS OF SOCIAL CHANGE

Here's to the crazy ones, the misfits, the rebels, the troublemakers, the round pegs in the square holes... the ones who see things differently — they're not fond of rules... You can quote them, disagree with them, glorify or vilify them, but the only thing you can't do is ignore them because they change things... they push the human race forward, and while some may see them as the crazy ones, we see genius, because the ones who are crazy enough to think that they can change the world, are the ones who do.

—Steve Jobs[1]

Motivators of social change, sometimes called the drivers of social change, **are the events, issues or concerns that trigger, drive, or force social change within a society.** Be careful! The motivators of social change are the prelude to the alteration of society. Motivators are the "why" of social change and not the actual social change.

For example, cell phones were simply a technological innovation until the innovation took the form of device convergence. This combined the capacities of several different gadgets—not only the telephone, but the camera, planner, watch, computer, music player, calculator, and more. Large numbers of people began using them for a wide variety of activities. This changed the way people communicate, buy and sell goods and services, share photographs and videos, manage their schedules, gather information, listen to music, and complete banking activities. The invention of cell phones—and the associated software applications—drove the change in society.

So what was the "why" of cell phones? What purposes did cell phones serve, and what motivated them to be produced? There are several reasons listed among the motivators that we will explore shortly. But consider first of all, in terms of functionalism discussed in the previous chapter, that society has various needs in order to survive and thrive. Communication is one of those needs and cell phones meet that need. There are also additional needs, including planning, purchasing, selling,

---

[1] Steve Jobs narrated the "Think Different" ad campaign for Apple in 1997, though of course the words came from a team of advertising professionals: https://fs.blog/2016/03/steve-jobs-crazy-ones/.

Cell phone technology has sped up the process of social change.

and even entertainment. Cell phones meet those needs as well, and even more. Some also argue that they might not meet some of those needs very well or that there are additional problems created by how they meet the needs, but the core fact is, the device exists and helps create social change—positive and negative alike—by doing what it does.

Now, shifting to the evolutionary perspective of social change, it takes time and effort to resolve all the needs of society. So isn't it easier if we make the process more efficient through the technology we have? As it turns out, as the saying had it in the first part of the 21st century, "there's an app for that." Literally. Instead of hauling around several different devices to help us accomplish all the different tasks we need to do, people like Steve Jobs imagined tools that allowed their users to complete many tasks. Through technology and device convergence, apparatuses such as cell phones participate in evolutionary social change as they create progress—at least in this respect.

Finally, in terms of the conflict perspective, competition and creativity between cell phone manufacturers help produce devices that not only do what their users want them to do, but do it at a price that the consumer is willing to pay. Devices that work well succeed, especially if their cost is relatively low, while gadgets that are all flash but lack substance or functionality fail. Through the technology of cell phones, social change comes about. The "how" is the story of Apple, Samsung, Motorola, and countless other producers, but the "why" is the social benefit or change that resulted from the development: improved efficiency and communication (at least as most people perceive it), in the case of cell phones.

As mentioned in the previous chapter, the "why" of social change helps us understand the "who." In the case of cell phones, the "who" is complex, since much of technology is a collective accomplishment to which many people and companies contributed. But among the most notable figures of the "who," Steve Jobs would qualify as one of the foremost visionaries.

Of course, cell phone technology and the push for efficiency and communication that motivated it are only the tip of the iceberg when we're talking about social change. Listed below are several motivators of social change. Though this list is extensive, it is certainly not complete. Also, many items on the list have complex connections to other items on the list:

- **Cultural shifts**

   Merriam-Webster.com defines *culture* as the customary beliefs, social forms, and material traits of a group of people, typically a racial, religious, or social group; and the set of shared attitudes, values, goals, and practices that characterizes an institution or organization. Cultural shifts might include changes in:
   - preferences and participation in the arts,
   - family, children, and intergenerational responsibilities,
   - gender roles and interactions in public and private,
   - patriarchal versus matriarchal practices,
   - financial habits (excess versus essentials) and generosity (philanthropy),
   - attitudes towards other groups of people (race, religion, sexual preference, nationality, etc.),
   - class (or caste) status, identities and relations,
   - child gender preferences,
   - inheritance (laws, processes and preferences),
   - forms of entertainment and leisure,
   - "pop culture" (fads),
   - formal versus casual, and
   - norms and morals.

- **Demographic changes**

   Demographics can be defined as the statistical characteristics of human populations (Merriam-Webster.com). Demographic changes might include the alteration of:
   - population size,
   - age of a population,
   - race and ethnicity of a population,
   - gender groups,
   - marital status,
   - educational levels,
   - employment and economic capacity of a population,
   - birth rates,
   - death rates, and
   - immigration and migration.

- **Economic restructuring**

Merriam-Webster.com defines *economic* as relating to or based on the production, distribution, and consumption of goods and services. Economic restructuring might include shifts in:

- income and distribution of wealth,
- socio-economic stratification (inequality),
- industrialization,
- globalization,
- economic development,
- real estate and housing cost/availability,
- market access,
- logistics,
- resource (natural and man-made) supply chains,
- consumerism and consumer choice,
- global and national recessions/depressions,
- trade agreements and embargos,
- taxes and tariffs,
- financial institutions and lending practices,
- stock market trends,
- multi-national corporations and small businesses,
- job market, and
- labor force (size, skill, pay, benefits, mobility, etc.).

- **Governmental and political activities**

Government can be defined as the people that constitute the governing authority of a political unit or organization; and the organization, machinery, or agency through which a political unit exercises authority and performs functions. *Political* can be defined as relating to, involving, or involved in politics, and especially party politics (Merriam-Webster.com). Changes in the governmental and political activities might include:

- election laws, methods, and results,
- taxation,

© Mattz90/Shutterstock.com

Social change can be triggered by the need for economic and tax reform. Economic issues and governmental activities are, of course, tightly intertwined.

- crime and corruption,
- governmental policy and laws,
- governmental spending,
- political parties and their agendas,
- military, veterans, and armament,
- wars, conflicts, and competition,
- national alliances and cooperation,
- assassinations of leadership,
- services (welfare, elder care, childcare, firefighting, infrastructure, etc.),
- terrorism,
- court rulings (producing judicial precedence),
- law enforcement and police practices,
- surveillance of citizens,
- treatment of intellectual property (patents, trademarks),
- emergency preparedness, and
- regulatory action.

- **Scientific and technological innovations**

  Merriam-Webster.com defines *innovation* as a new idea, method, or device. Scientific and technological innovations might include:
  - scientific theories,
  - scientific instrumentation and data collection,
  - space and ocean exploration,
  - engineering design, materials, and methods,
  - new devices and consumer products,
  - computerization, automation, and artificial intelligence,
  - genetically modified organisms / GMO foods,
  - cloning (human and non-human),
  - health care:
    - telemedicine,
    - immunizations,
    - prosthetics,
    - surgical procedures and medical testing,
    - pharmaceuticals and treatment plans,
    - disease and pandemics,
    - stem cell applications, and
    - DNA manipulation;

- environmental concerns (natural or man-made):
    - o pollution,
    - o over-population and overuse of resources,
    - o climate change,
    - o renewable resources and energy,
    - o natural disasters (earthquakes, wildfires, hurricanes, etc.),
    - o pest control (mosquitos, flies, snakes, bats, and rats),
    - o species extinction,
    - o weed and invasive species control, and
    - o man-made disasters (oil spills, global warming, dam failure, etc.);
- media, communications, and internet access:
    - o fees,
    - o 24/7 local and global news,
    - o social media,
    - o governmental control, censorship, and filtering,
    - o hacking,
    - o educational programming,
    - o advertising,
    - o free press (political critics/pundits/analysts), and
    - o the entertainment industry.

- **Social-institutional shifts**

Social institutions can be defined as an established somewhat public organization or corporation, such as a bank or university (Merriam-Webster.com). Shifts within social institutions might include:
- educational developments:
    - o access for girls and minorities,
    - o increased/decreased graduation rates,
    - o literacy rates,
    - o public school, private school, homeschooling,
    - o educational curriculum,
    - o higher education, and
    - o intellectual freedom;
- professional organizations' shifting agendas,
- development and participation in charitable organizations and clubs,
- access and quality of health care:
    - o cost structure and health insurance,
    - o mental and behavioral health care,

- o emergency health care services,
- o elder care, and
- o prenatal and women's health care (including birth control);
- changes in religious institutions' (churches'):
  - o practices,
  - o thoughts/doctrine/teachings,
  - o membership, and
  - o leadership.

Religious concerns are last on this list, but as the saying goes, definitely not least. We advocate that they deserve to be not only explored in more detail, but they require a great deal more attention as motivators of social change. This is true on organizational, group, and individual levels. Religion certainly interconnects with each of the other main bullet points—cultural shifts, demographic changes, economic restructuring, governmental and political activities, scientific and technological innovations, and social-institutional shifts—and may combine with each of those other motivators of social change as well as acting on its own to spark or drive social change. This will become increasingly evident as we proceed.

Members and friends of the Boise Episcopal Church marched in the city's Pride Parade in June 2016 in support of the local LGBT community.

A motivator of social change may be a one-time event or issue, but more likely, it is a small step in a continuing process that pushes social change further down the road of a long-term alteration of society. For example, events such as the removal of the Berlin Wall[2] and the election of US President Barack Obama[3] may appear to have been social change in and of themselves, but these events were, in fact, outward expressions of an extensive social change process that had already begun within a segment of society prior to the event that brought the change to the entire society.

Sometimes, social change is a backlash or negative response to the original motivating event or issue. For example, as part of the complex social movement today known as the Arab Spring[4] (starting in mid-December 2010, but with some sustained related events continuing until 2014), the Shi'a people of Bahrain took to the streets in protest, attempting to gain more political freedom. However, instead of expanding rights and freedoms, the Bahraini government declared a state of emergency and martial law. The uprising in Bahrain was crushed with police and military personnel from Saudi Arabia and the UAE. Thousands of Bahraini citizens were arrested, and Shi'a mosques were bulldozed (NPR 2012; Al Jazeera 2011; BBC 2014). As a result of their demand for more political freedom, the Shi'a people lost, at least temporarily, what little political power and freedoms they had in Bahrain.

The motivators listed above can bring a change in thoughts, habits, convictions, attitudes, and social norms. These changes may well initiate a domino effect in which one change brings another, and that change brings another, and so on and so on. These motivators may cause violent action or cooperative change. They may also bring leaders to light who might otherwise have stayed outside of the public eye. In later chapters, we will discuss a few of these organizations, groups, and individuals. But first, we need to define "religious faith" and discuss the religious landscape across the globe, as we will do in the next two following chapters.

---

[2] The Berlin Wall first began to open up in 1989, almost inadvertently, and was finally demolished in 1991. Most historians cite this as a signature event in ending the "Cold War" between the United States and the Soviet Union. For additional information about the fall of the Berlin Wall and its Cold War importance, go to https://www.history.com/topics/cold-war/berlin-wall or to https://hub.jhu.edu/2019/11/05/berlin-wall-mary-elise-sarotte/.

[3] The election of Barack Obama as the first African-American president of the United States has been widely acclaimed as a key landmark in American history. For biographies of Barack and Michelle Obama, go to: https://barackobama.com/about/. For the website of The Obama Presidential Center and the Obama Foundation, go to https://www.obama.org/.

[4] The Arab Spring social movement by most accounts started with protests in Tunisia and Egypt over the horrific deaths of two young men in each country that occurred closely together. The unrest spread quickly—fueled and hosted by social media—to many countries across the Middle East. The social change that resulted included regime change in Tunisia, Egypt and Libya, and sustained reform protests in Syria, Yemen, Bahrain, and other nations. For more on the Arab Spring, see https://www.npr.org/2011/12/17/143897126/the-arab-spring-a-year-of-revolution and https://rlp.hds.harvard.edu/faq/arab-spring-egypt.

Alden: I wanted to ask for your thoughts about America's unrest in 2020 resulting from several well-documented police killings of Black Americans over the previous several years, including George Floyd, Botham Jean, Stephon Clark, and Breonna Taylor.

Cynthia: Well, let me start by saying emphatically that I absolutely disagree with those who want to force social change through violence! Violence will not solve anything and will likely make the situation worse. We don't need a race war. In war, the enemy is typically dehumanized, and haven't we had enough of that? In fact, what we need is racial justice and equality!

Alden: Have you protested during this recent unrest?

Cynthia: Of course! My eldest son and I protested with friends in a 3-mile march in our hometown a week after George Floyd's death. I want racial justice across America, but particularly, I want racial justice in the town where my grandchild lives!

In fact, while marching and singing *"Amazing Grace"* with people of all races, ages and genders, I saw another middle-aged white woman carrying a sign that said,

"I see you!

I value you!

I stand with you!

You matter!"

Wow! What a wonderful message! As I stood there letting her message sink in, an older Black woman stopped next to me to read the sign, and she said, "I've been doing this for 50 years. You'd think that we'd eventually get this thing right!" "Yes!" I agreed, and added, "I think the time has finally come that people's hearts and minds are deeply feeling the pain of injustice. Change is happening!" The older Black woman smiled through her coronavirus mask and sang, "Praise Jesus! Amazing grace, how sweet the sound...!"

Alden: Do you honestly see racial justice in America's future?

Cynthia: Yes, I do! There is serious, wide-spread, grassroots desire within America to see justice and dignity for all people!

A student recently asked me if I thought that Dr. King's dream was dying. The question broke my heart, but I took a slow deep breath and responded, "In fact, I think that Dr. King's dream is more alive today than ever! And you have a role in that dream!"

* The views we express in these conversations are our own as private citizens and are not meant to represent the perspectives or policies of any other person, social group, or institution, including those of the religious organizations we attend or of our employer.

DEFINING "RELIGIOUS FAITH"

Religious suffering is, at one and the same time, the expression of real suffering and a protest against real suffering. Religion is the sigh of the oppressed creature, the heart of a heartless world, and the soul of soulless conditions. It is the opium of the people.

—*Karl Marx*[1]

Defining "religious faith" is both simple and complicated. It's simple because we seem to have an intuitive understanding of what religious faith is all about. It's complicated because we not only have an intuitive understanding of religious faith, but also various life experiences that inform our intuitive understandings tremendously. This makes defining the term more difficult than we might at first believe. So, as we explore the definition of religious faith, readers should be aware of how their own experiences and encounters with religion shape their understanding of "religion" and "faith" alike.

Let's start by establishing that religious faith is of course a religious phenomenon. People who belong to a particular religion have chosen a religious faith, also known as church affiliation or membership. In other words, someone's religious faith can essentially mean **where they have decided to go to church.** In the following pages, we will discuss this particular aspect of religious faith in a little more detail. Of course, there has to be more to the story of why religious faith motivates particular people to participate in or bring about social change. If simply going to church led people to create social change, more religious people would be doing exactly that. Our world would be a much different place if mere church membership and attendance led to social change. Though we will survey the religious landscape in Chapter 4, there has to be—and is—more to the concept of religious faith than mere membership or church attendance alone.

---

[1] Of course, Marx was no friend of religion per se; in fact, in the text that followed this famous remark, Marx characterized religion as an illusion that should be destroyed. Still, his statement is relevant to the role of religion in social change. His full comments: https://www.marxists.org/archive/marx/works/1843/critique-hpr/intro.htm.

Religious faith is part of the human experience and exists in many shapes and forms.

To begin to define "religious faith," let's start with the term "religion." This can also be a complicated issue. An eminent scholar of religion, Ronald Johnstone (2006), takes several pages to define the term, walking the reader through the meaning of the Latin *religare* (a tie that binds), substantive and functional considerations, an extensive discussion of religion as a group phenomenon, and associated factors such as beliefs, practices, moral prescriptions, and a view of the sacred. Then invoking Peter Berger's discussion of religion as a "sacred canopy" (1990) intended to shield believers in a chaotic world that threatens place in society and even identity itself, Johnstone proposes an essential definition of religion that will also work for our purposes in this book:

> *Religion is a set of beliefs and rituals by which a group of people seeks to understand, explain, and deal with a world of complexity, uncertainty, and mystery, by identifying a sacred canopy of explanation and reassurance under which to live (2006, 14).*

In defining religion in this way, it's also important to note that, along with Johnstone, we consider spirituality as an inherent component of religious belief and behavior. Unlike some modern critics of organized religion who see a stark difference between religion and spirituality, we believe both potentially enfold the other. The ideas of the sacred, supernatural, mythological, psychological, emotional, what the venerable German theologian Rudolf Otto long ago called the *mysterium tremendum* (1923), and so forth are relevant to religion rather than distinct from it. We do, however, recognize that group processes and other organizational factors can in some religious contexts appear to or actually take precedence over spiritual concerns. In such cases, believers who see the situation in this way may indeed find more satisfaction in exploring individual spirituality than in participating in the organization.

Moreover, as in the preface, we also recognize that religion can have distinctly negative aspects, to the point of "turning off" or even traumatizing some believers. We have not explored these issues at length, since we are not experts in the relevant fields of deviance, terrorism, religious conflict, cult behavior, and so forth. Accordingly, our focus in this book has generally been on religion's pro-social aspects, but we point out the downsides of religious belief and behavior when relevant.

One such instance is Karl Marx' well-known discussion of religion as "the opium of the people" (1844). His precise meaning has often been debated, but read in context in Marx' critique of Hegelian philosophy, Marx believed religion was often an instrument used by those in power to pacify relatively powerless believers. If the *bourgeoisie* (upper class) could persuade the *proletariat* (lower class) to simply consent to their station in life, then life would continue as normal. Note as well that opium is a sedative, which was Marx' point: Religion soothes and sedates believers, who then accept their place in society and the accompanying oppression.

Many scholars and observers of Marx see this statement as valid. However, if this is true of all religious people everywhere, quite candidly, there's really no point to this book. People who believe in religion would merely accept their place in the world around us. Then life would go on with a lot of singing and praying, especially when its experiences got difficult, but otherwise unchanged. If Marx's observation holds true on an individual level of analysis, religious individuals also would not try to change their circumstances.

But is this always the case? Part of what we are exploring in this book is the distinct possibility that Marx oversimplified the relationship between religion and social change. Certainly, one point Marx made remains indisputable: Religion provides a great deal of comfort to those who believe, reassures them, and gives them meaning in their lives. But is it possible that some religious believers actually don't submissively accept their station in life and are instead inspired by religion to *actively make changes* instead of passively accept the status quo?

Later in this book, we will explore the logical and experiential case for this—or in other words, we will not only explore why this could be the case, but also meet people whose religion motivates them to advocate for change. As pointed out in previous chapters, the "why" seems to select and motivate the "who." Not only are there many historical examples of religiously motivated individuals who have engaged in social change, but religious concerns are still motivating some individuals to work for a better world.

One of the "superpowers" of religion in this regard is socialization, or the way people learn to become members of a given religious group. Socialization involves how and what believers learn about any given religion cognitively, behaviorally, and socially, and we will gradually explore the role of socialization as we examine the "who" and "why" of how religion participates in motivating social change. In basic terms of religion, socialization is Sunday School lessons and worship services, chants and mantras, scriptures and religious commentaries, rituals and observances, prayers, fasting, meditating, spiritual experiences, tithing or other donations, listening to or singing hymns or devotional music, service and outreach activities, proselyting work, and even going to religion-sponsored social events (Sherkat 2003).

Faith is sometimes characterized as a trusting step forward into the unknown or a "leap of faith."

Through socialization, believers—the "who"—find out what they are supposed to do, how they are supposed to think about it, and (at least to some extent) why this is. Socialization contributes not only a sense of desired behavior and attitude, but also a way of thinking about the behaviors and attitudes—in short, a worldview, also called *weltanschauung* in German. Importantly, socialization is a participatory process rather than a mere procedure of indoctrination or inculcation, and believers being socialized make active sense of the information they receive (Klingenberg and Sjö 2019; see also https://open.lib.umn.edu/sociology/part/chapter-4-socialization/ and https://open.lib.umn.edu/sociology/chapter/17-3-sociological-perspectives-on-religion/). In short: Religion contributes to social change through socialization.

With the term "religion" explained, we turn to a discussion of "faith." What is faith? In modern American society, faith is often used interchangeably with terms such as trust, confidence, and belief, which we note are hallmarks of socialized attitudes and behavior. Faith is also described as acting without a complete knowledge in uncertain or even in dangerous circumstances. Then again, the Urban Dictionary has a completely different meaning for "Faith," which is a label that describes "a stunningly gorgeous, cute, all-around girl with a dazzling smile and hypnotic eyes." (See the original entry at https://www.urbandictionary.com/define.php?term=Faith; spelling and usage updated.) This concept clearly has a wide range of meaning in popular usage.

So again, what is faith? Several more traditional definitions based on thought from religious leaders and gifted writers spring to mind.

> *Faith is like Wi-Fi. It's invisible, but it has the power to connect you to what you need.*
> —Anonymous[2]

---

[2] This anonymous motivational quote is used in several sources throughout the traditional Christian context and tracing it back to its original author is difficult if not impossible at this point.

Faith is taking the first step even when you don't see the whole staircase.
—Marian Wright Edelman, attributing the quote to Dr. Martin Luther King Jr.[3]

Faith is the bird that feels the light when the dawn is still dark.
—Rabindranath Tagore, poet from India.
(*https://www.brainyquote.com/quotes/rabindranath_tagore_121379*)

Faith is not belief without proof, but trust without reservation.
—D. Elton Trueblood, American theologian. (*https://www.quotes.net/quote/18132*)

Faith is a passionate intuition.
—William Wordsworth, English poet.
(*https://www.brainyquote.com/authors/william-wordsworth-quotes*)

What does it profit, my brethren, if someone says he has faith but does not have works? Can faith save him? If a brother or sister is naked and destitute of daily food, and one of you says to them, "Depart in peace, be warmed and filled," but you do not give them the things which are needed for the body, what does it profit? Thus also faith by itself, if it does not have works, is dead. But someone will say, "You have faith, and I have works." Show me your faith without your works, and I will show you my faith by my works...For as the body without the spirit is dead, so faith without works is dead also.
—New Testament, James 2:14-18, 26 (New King James Version)

Merriam-Webster's dictionary (https://www.merriam-webster.com) further provides us with a complex definition of faith:

noun: 1. a. allegiance to duty or person;
b. fidelity to one's promises, sincerity of intentions;
2. a. belief and trust in and loyalty to God, belief in the traditional doctrines of a religion;
b. firm belief in something for which there is no proof, complete trust; and
3. something that is believed especially with strong conviction.

verb: believe, trust

Further definitions of faith from Dictionary.com (https://www.dictionary.com) and Vocabulary.com (https://www.vocabulary.com) also underscore various dimensions of this term that provide a full definition of faith, including the aspects of confidence and trust, belief without proof, loyalty and fidelity, putting belief into action, and even the sense of a system of religious belief or membership.

Of course, not all faith is religious faith. Many people place their faith in themselves, science, nature, society, nation (and government), family (and ancestors), friends, doctors and medical science (or NOT doctors and medicine, as with some in the era of the COVID pandemic), and time-honored

---

[3] This quote is frequently attributed to Dr. King today, but according to the discussion at https://quoteinvestigator.com/2019/04/18/staircase/#note-135686-5, several versions of this idea existed well before King and this exact quote isn't found in his published works. It seems most reasonable to credit American writer Marian Wright Edelman, who both attributed the quote to King and claimed to hear him say it directly. See also Reynolds, Barbara A. (ed.), 1988. *And Still We Rise: Interviews With 50 Black Role Models*. Washington D.C.: USA Today Books (Gannett). See pp. 73-75.

Faith, specifically religious faith, is a complex idea, but one that is typically easy to identify when it is placed into action.

written words of wisdom, such as the US Constitution and Bill of Rights. They may even place their faith in sports teams! As in Edward Bailey's concept of "implicit religion" (2011), faith as we know it today can extend to a wide variety of the human experience rather than religion alone. Consequently, thought and behavior that resembles religion (or is religion simply the most-recognized form of these cognitive-behavioral tendencies?) can emerge in a wide variety of social contexts. We will discuss more about the significance of implicit religion in later segments.

In any case, since there are so many different ways of looking at "faith," it seems understandable to be a bit frustrated by this point when trying to pull them all together into a coherent statement. However, we can still synthesize those various aspects of faith into a working definition. The multiple dimensions of faith listed above, especially those that specifically involve religion, all suggest that it leads to **a behavioral outcome of the individual's or group's trust, confidence, and belief**. Faith—active confidence, active trust, active loyalty, and so forth—is the motivating factor behind the "works" (in James' words found in the Bible), or the active practice of religion.

Thus faith—especially as used in the religious context by James—is what produces the action of religious belief, not merely a cognitive-intuitive ideal. Faith can be considered the difference between believing that someone who is naked and hungry should be clothed and fed, and actually **making the decision** to clothe and feed someone. Then the individual with faith **does so**. Faith is not only what believers trust, place their confidence in, or feel loyalty towards—it is what they decide to DO in response to that trust, confidence, loyalty, and so forth. Synthesizing those ideas, we find that:

> *Religious faith is belief, trust in, and loyalty to God or a supernatural power, and/or belief in the traditional doctrines, teachings, or system of a religion, which often motivates individual and group behavior.*

Given that definition, this quote makes sense:

> *Some time ago someone likened [religious] faith to the wind: we cannot see the wind, we cannot hear the wind unless it blows against something, we can only feel the wind when it touches our skin or rustles our hair. Faith is like that wind. We cannot see what we believe in, we cannot hear what we believe in unless we open our eyes to the truth, but we can sure feel that our faith is justified by the joy we feel in our hearts.* (https://www.allaboutreligion.org).

We will carry forward with that idea of religious faith: The belief and worldview that motivates an individual to live life and move forward. The individual with religious faith will see the world in a particular way due to religious socialization and be inclined to make active decisions according to that faith. This is the "why" that we can expect to motivate the "who."

In summary, as previously mentioned, one of the commonly used senses of "faith" is simply religious membership. Although we are defining religious faith essentially as a worldview put into action from a smaller collective if not individual standpoint, it is nonetheless important when considering this issue in general to understand the religious landscape and the "religious faiths" it contains—AND the commonalities between most major religions in today's world. This should help us to understand the variety of possible motivations of believers, as well as the commonalities between the various "faiths" that contribute to social change.

Notes from the Authors*

Cynthia: Alden, religious faith is a fascinating area, especially when connected to social change. What does religious faith mean to you?

Alden: To me, as we've defined it in this chapter, faith is not only believing but also acting. It's said in the Bible that faith the size of a mustard seed can move mountains. But as far as I've ever seen, mountains don't just move if you sit there and stare at them, hoping they decide to get up and go. You might have to grab a shovel yourself and help the mountain start moving.

The funny thing is, other people may well then see you working and decide to help. If you get people with the heavy equipment, they come in and suddenly the mountain starts moving in large chunks. Faith eventually moves the mountain—people just have to decide they're going to get started and work together to move it. It's like planting the mustard seed, watering it, then watching it sprout and take root. Eventually it grows into a large plant that bears useful seeds of its own. But the work of planting the seed and getting the plant to grow has to happen first. That's the way I've seen faith move mountains, anyway.

Cynthia: Yes, true. It sounds like you've been involved in social change of your own. How has your faith played a role in that?

(Continued)

Alden: Well, I've never quite been the protest-march type, though George Floyd's death may have flipped the switch on that. More often, my social change efforts have come by obnoxiously expressing my opinions on social media. But I did get directly involved a few years ago dealing with a local privately run utility that … well, let's just say, many of my neighbors and I thought they needed to make some improvements.

It's a long and complicated story, but three neighbors and I actually ended up volunteering to represent our community's interests in front of the Arizona Corporation Commission and administrative law judge—and the decision that resulted was in our community's best interests. Curiously, as people of faith—yet different faiths!—we still had the sense that we had been intended to be at that place at that time. It's also interesting that, most of us who led out on this effort ran into various difficulties and couldn't sustain our roles. But others in our community picked up where we left off. It still took a few years, but due to the involvement of others in the community, that same state commission later ended up taking corrective action against that utility company.

My current interests in social change come from my deep and abiding feeling that those of us who believe that God is love and loves all people the same have no justification at all in mistreating each other. I have spoken up to advocate for refugees, children who have been forcibly separated from their parents, those of other religious traditions that are frequently misunderstood (including Muslims, Sikhs, and Jews), those afflicted with depression and anxiety (including LGBT people), and most notably Black individuals and other people of color. Three decades ago, I lived in a largely Black population in the Caribbean for two years serving a religious mission, and it forever altered my perspective on minorities and Black people in particular. Race relations and religion in America have a long and sad history. My own church, like many others but also with a handful of challenges unique to itself, has had a problematic background with understanding and including Black people. I am actively working to understand and change this as well. From a "God is love" perspective, this seems only fitting.

---

* The views we express in these conversations are our own as private citizens and are not meant to represent the perspectives or policies of any other person, social group, or institution, including those of the religious organizations we attend or of our employer.

CHAPTER 4

THE RELIGIOUS LANDSCAPE AND COMMON RELIGIOUS PRINCIPLES

God has given us many faiths but only one world in which to co-exist. May your work help all of us to cherish our commonalities and feel enlarged by our differences.

—*Rabbi Lord Jonathan Sacks*[1]

As we consider the meaning of religious faith and its role as a motivator of social change, we also need to be able to understand the wide variety of religious traditions in our world today. As we consider the major world religions in the world today, we will see both how many people belong to the various groups as well as note some commonalities between them. For instance, many Christians may be surprised to find that "The Golden Rule" (do unto others as you would have others do unto you) didn't originate with the New Testament. This idea actually predates the advent of Christianity, which likely acquired The Golden Rule from Judaism, though a version of this idea also exists in Buddhism and yet others. In any case, examining the landscape of religious belief will help facilitate our understanding of religion and social change alike.

In this chapter, we will examine the world's major religions, starting with those with at least a billion members, as well as discuss some common themes between those major religions. We will discuss twelve major religious identities, as well as several others that have historical prominence or contemporary influence. As we do, we will see that—as Rabbi Sacks points out—the world's major religions have commonalities that underlie their differences and can play a role in bringing believers together. The common religious principles also help motivate the "who" of social change: the individuals who feel inspired to act according to beliefs that are commonly accepted by most people in the world today.

As of the early twenty-first century, these are the most populated religious groups in the world (Tables 1, 2, and 3)—those that have at least a documented million members, as well as several others that are well worth mentioning (Tables 4 and 5). Our tables of religions were inspired by a somewhat similar

---

[1] The late Rabbi Lord Jonathan Sacks—knighted in 2005 and given many other honors from Jewish and interfaith groups—lived in England and dedicated his life to promoting peace and understanding between religions. This quote can be found at https://www.azquotes.com/quotes/topics/commonality.html.

list compiled at https://www.theregister.co.uk/2006/10/06/the_odd_body_religion/. However, that original list, created in 2006, required some updates in terms of categories and numbers, in one case also correcting a substantial overestimation.

The global population estimates given in this chapter are approximations rather than a precise census. They are drawn from various sources, as indicated in the tables below. Reasonably reliable population estimates for religious subgroups have been listed when available. Estimates for the billion-member groups are rounded to the nearest 100M and those for the million-member groups are rounded to the nearest 1M, except for self-reporting groups, which are rounded to the nearest 100K. Estimates are drawn from data gathered between 2010 and 2020 whenever possible. We have made every effort to try to establish estimates that are likely current as of 2020, with distinct preference given to Pew research data.

Table 1: The Billion-Member Religions

Rank	Religious Category	Population Estimates
1	**Christianity**,[2] including Catholic (ab. 1.1B),[3] Protestant and non-denominational Christian (ab. 800M),[4] Eastern Orthodox (ab. 260M)[5], LDS (16.5M),[6] Jehovah's Witnesses (8.7M)[7], Christian Scientists (>1M),[8] and others.	2.3 billion
2	**Islam**,[9] including all subgroups within Sunni (ab. 1.5B) and Shi'a (ab. 250M) major divisions, and a few others such as the Ahmadi (likely ab. 10M)[10] not fitting precisely in either.	1.8 billion
3	**Unaffiliated**,[11] including "spiritual but not religious" and other consciously independent religious believers of multiple traditions, as well as secularists, agnostics, and atheists.	1.2 billion
4	**Hinduism**,[12] including Vaishnavism (ab. 744M), Shaivism (ab. 293M), Shaktism (ab. 35M), and smaller movements like neo-Hinduism and reform Hinduism (estimates not given).	1.1 billion

[2] The groups included under Christianity are according to Pew Research Center's grouping. Data for the estimates were drawn from different studies done at different times, so figures reported for some Christian groups in some studies conflict with those given in others. Estimates for smaller Christian organizations are self-reported.

[3] 2015 Pew statistics. See https://www.pewresearch.org/fact-tank/2017/04/05/christians-remain-worlds-largest-religious-group-but-they-are-declining-in-europe/. The Catholic Communion actually claims a higher membership across the churches of its various rites of about 1.33 billion; we are using the Pew estimate for mere mathematical consistency. Under a more generous estimate, the actual number of Christians globally may be around 2.5 billion.

[4] 2011 Pew statistics. https://www.pewforum.org/2011/12/19/global-christianity-traditions/#protestant

[5] 2017 Pew statistics. https://www.pewforum.org/2017/11/08/orthodox-christianity-in-the-21st-century/

[6] Self-reported. LDS membership figure current as of June 2020. https://newsroom.churchofjesuschrist.org/facts-and-statistics/country/united-states#

[7] Self-reported. Jehovah's Witnesses membership figure current as of June 2020. Members and interested friends self-reported as high as 20M. https://www.jw.org/en/jehovahs-witnesses/faq/how-many-jw/

[8] This small but historically influential Christian tradition has not published official statistics since claiming 268K members in 1946. Current estimates range from 100K to 400K. http://www.thearda.com/Denoms/D_1126.asp, https://www.pbs.org/wnet/religionandethics/2008/08/01/christian-science-healing/6/

[9] 2015 Pew statistics. See https://www.pewresearch.org/fact-tank/2017/04/05/christians-remain-worlds-largest-religious-group-but-they-are-declining-in-europe/. No precise counts of Sunni, Shi'a, and other groups are available, but religious demographers estimate about 87% of Muslims are Sunni, 12% Shi'a, and 1% other. A study at https://www.pewforum.org/2015/04/02/religious-projections-2010-2050/ further projects that Islam is growing faster than Christianity and may overtake it sometime in the next few decades, possibly even as soon as 2050.

Buddhist monks with elephant.

Table 2: The Hundred-Million-Member Religions

Rank	Religious Category	Population Estimates
5	**Buddhism,**[13] including Mahayana (ab. 200M), Theraveda (ab. 133M), and Vajrayana or Tibetan traditions (ab. 21M), as well as several smaller groups. These population subgroup estimates are approximations illustrative of the comparative proportions within Buddhism.[14]	500M
6	**Traditional "folk" religions,**[15] including Daoism and Confucianism in China, as well as African, Native American, and Australian aboriginal native religious worship. Spiritism can also be considered in this category. This does NOT include African diaspora religions, which are listed later.	418M

[10] Estimates for the Ahmadiyya sect vary widely; 10M is a realistic educated guess. See this BBC religion report (http://news.bbc.co.uk/2/hi/south_asia/8711026.stm) for more details about the sect, often seen within Islam as heretical.

[11] 2015 Pew statistics. See https://www.pewresearch.org/fact-tank/2017/04/05/christians-remain-worlds-largest-religious-group-but-they-are-declining-in-europe/. Worldwide estimates of the unaffiliated are approximations.

[12] *Ibid.*; see also 2012 Pew statistics at https://www.pewforum.org/2012/12/18/global-religious-landscape-hindu/. The Hare Krishna sect of Hinduism, which is relatively well-known in North America, is part of the larger Vaishnavism tradition. Pew researchers are reluctant to endorse proportions; extrapolations of estimates are from religious demographers Johnson and Grim. See Johnson, Todd M., and Brian J. Grim. 2013. *The World's Religions in Figures: An Introduction to International Religious Demography.* Malden, MA: John Wiley and Sons.

[13] 2015 Pew statistics. See https://www.pewresearch.org/fact-tank/2017/04/05/christians-remain-worlds-largest-religious-group-but-they-are-declining-in-europe/. The overall Buddhist population estimate is reasonably reliable.

[14] According to this 2012 Pew statistical report (https://www.pewforum.org/2012/12/18/global-religious-landscape-buddhist/), demographers have had a great deal of trouble establishing the precise size of the various Buddhist sub-traditions. Key contributing factors include overlap between traditions AND inaccessibility or lack of concrete data such as population counts and census surveys. So the figures shown should be considered representative of the relative sizes and proportions of Buddhist subgroups based on extrapolations given in https://berkleycenter.georgetown.edu/essays/demographics-of-buddhism, not actual population counts. Zen Buddhism, arguably the best-known form of Buddhism in America, is part of the Mahayana tradition.

[15] 2017 Pew statistics. See https://www.pewforum.org/2017/04/05/the-changing-global-religious-landscape/. This is the source for the 418 million population figure. A previous Pew research report in 2012 estimating 405 million (https://www.pewforum.org/2012/12/18/global-religious-landscape-folk/) further notes the difficulty of measuring this particular category, particularly in China. The 2012 report also elaborates on traditional and folk religions globally. Given the discrepancy between the two estimates, we opted for the more recent figure.

Table 3: The Million-Member Religions

Rank	Religious Category	Population Estimates
7	**Sikhism,**[16] which originated in India in the fifteenth century, advocates equality for all people and teaches that all people have divinity within.	25M
8	**Juche,**[17] or formalized North Korean nationalist ideology, is centered on the nation and its leaders alike and seems to operate much like a religion.	+/- 25M
9	**Judaism,**[18] including Orthodox, Conservative, and Reform general types. Some 350K Messianic Jews also exist, but are not often accepted by other groups as authentically Jewish.[19]	15M
10	**Baha'i,**[20] originating in nineteenth century Iran, is a group now found globally. The Baha'i accept all faiths as valid and are preparing themselves and the world for a coming era of peace.	More than 5M
11	**Jainism,**[21] originating in India in the sixth century BC, practices a rigorous lifestyle of *ahims*a (nonviolence), including a vegan diet, and other ascetic practices.	More than 4M
12	**Shinto,**[22] a Japanese-centered religion originating in the eighth century BC, has profoundly influenced that land's culture over time but is now today claimed by a mere minority.	3M

---

[16] 2015 Pew statistics. See https://www.pewforum.org/2015/04/02/other-religions/. The Pew estimate may err on the conservative side, as some population estimates give the actual number of Sikhs as high as 30 million.

[17] Worldometers. See https://www.worldometers.info/world-population/north-korea-population/#:~:text=North%20Korea%202020%20population%20is,(and%20dependencies)%20by%20population. *Juche*, pronounced "joo-shay," is usually translated as "self-reliance," according to the idea that the Democratic People's Republic of Korea is a nation unto itself. *Juche* is required of all approximately 25 million DPRK citizens (hence the estimate), though some are likely more dedicated than others to this ideology.

[18] 2015 Pew statistics. See https://www.pewforum.org/2015/04/02/jews/. Our estimate rounds up from 14.7M. The categorization of Jewish subgroups is based on 2016 Pew statistics. See https://www.pewresearch.org/fact-tank/2016/03/15/unlike-u-s-few-jews-in-israel-identify-as-reform-or-conservative/. These groups often differ geographically—as with the prevalence of Reform Jews in the United States, more than elsewhere in the world—and Israeli Jewish groups do not necessarily correspond to their counterparts elsewhere in the world. Due to the complexity of local variation, as well as lack of global data regarding self-identification, we have made no attempt to estimate the relative sizes and proportions of Jewish subgroups.

[19] *The Atlantic*, 2012. See https://www.theatlantic.com/international/archive/2012/11/kosher-jesus-messianic-jews-in-the-holy-land/265670/. Messianic Jews are rather controversial in the more traditional sectors of Judaism due to their acceptance of Jesus Christ as the Jewish Messiah.

[20] 2015 Pew statistics. See https://www.pewforum.org/2015/04/02/other-religions/. Some observers place Baha'i global membership as high as 7 million, but we are giving benefit of the doubt to the Pew estimate.

[21] *Ibid.* Some observers suggest the true number of Jains may remain officially undercounted because some Jains also self-identify as Hindu on surveys, censuses, and other demographic data sources.

[22] *Ibid.* Some estimates of Shinto are as high as 5 million, but without formal membership records, a firm way of distinguishing Shinto from non-Shinto (no rituals are required to join), and the fact that an unknown number of Japanese practice both Buddhism and Shinto, we acknowledge the possibility but remain with the Pew estimate.

Woman praying at sunset.

Table 4: Likely Million-Member Religions

Religious Category	Population Estimates[23]
Cao Dai,[24] a Vietnamese New Religious Movement, is highly eclectic and borrows substantially from seemingly almost all the previously mentioned religious groups.	+/- 3M
Tenrikyo,[25] a Japanese New Religious Movement, subscribes to the teachings of Nakayama Miki, who believers consider to be the revelator of God.	+/- 2M
Druze,[26] a Middle Eastern sect originating in the eleventh century, is concentrated in Syria and Lebanon and emphasizes philosophy and spiritual purity.	1M

[23] Since the population estimates of many of these religions—and also most of those following in Table 5—vary widely and valid/accurate membership estimates are hard to generate, we caution that these population counts are highly approximate. For the same reason, we have abandoned the numerical ranking of these religious groups at this point.

[24] Encyclopedia.com. https://www.encyclopedia.com/philosophy-and-religion/other-religious-beliefs-and-general-terms/miscellaneous-religion/cao-dai. Estimates of Cao Dai membership vary widely, ranging anywhere from 2 to 7 million, though most authoritative sources seem to trend on the lower end. So the given figure of 3 million seems like a reasonably safe conservative estimate.

[25] Worldatlas. See https://www.worldatlas.com/articles/what-is-tenriism-tenrikyo.html. The previously cited 2015 Pew research article for many of the other religious groups, https://www.pewforum.org/2015/04/02/other-religions/, mentions Tenrikyo among significant religious groups but declines to estimate membership. Around 2 million is our safe conservative educated guess.

[26] 2016 Pew statistics. See https://www.pewresearch.org/fact-tank/2016/03/21/5-facts-about-israeli-druze-a-unique-religious-and-ethnic-group/. Given the challenges the Druze face throughout the Middle East, some observers believe the embattled historic religious group may be approaching extinction. For this perspective and more on the Druze in general, see https://www.washingtoninstitute.org/fikraforum/view/druze-communities-face-a-regional-decline-in-influence.

Rastafarian dredlocks.

© Maria Bobrova/Shutterstock.com

Table 5: Likely Less than a Million or Population Unknown

Unitarian Universalism,[27] a highly eclectic liberal-leaning religious group based in Boston, has no formal creed and accepts beliefs of all different types of religions. Formal membership statistics are kept for US congregations (ab. 153K in 2019), while informal global estimates range as high as 800K.

Rastafarianism[28] is a New Religious Movement found throughout the Caribbean, particularly Jamaica, and other areas of the world with substantial Black populations. Beliefs range from the divinity of man to Blacks being the true House of Israel who will one day return to Ethiopia, the Promised Land. There is no official Rastafarian central organization, but membership is estimated at between 700K to 1M.

African diaspora religions[29] originated with roots in traditional African religions such as Vodun and Yoruba but were transformed by their new cultural environments as well as surrounding religious influences, often including spiritism and Roman Catholicism. These include Vodou in the Caribbean (particularly Haiti) and Louisiana in the US, Santeria in Cuba and Latin America, and Candomblé in Brazil, to name a few. Reliable estimates of the population actively practicing them are unknown.

Neo-paganism and Wicca,[30] sometimes known as "New Age," involve the worship of a god and goddess along with various fertility rituals, energy healing, and magic. Estimates are difficult to generate; demographer Ethan Doyle White merely estimates hundreds of thousands worldwide.

Zoroastrianism,[31] dating from the sixth century BC in Iran and Persia, is small in number today but thought to be historically influential in terms of ancient Judaism, Christianity, and Islam. Concepts such as free will, eternal struggle between two beings personifying good and evil, a day of judgment, and others may have descended from this religious tradition. Estimates of current numbers of Zoroastrians vary from 100K to 200K, with the number thought to be declining due to their ongoing persecution in Iran, where Zoroastrians are the most concentrated.

[27] Statistics for US Unitarian Universalism membership are self-reported. See https://www.uua.org/data/demographics/uua-statistics and https://www.learnreligions.com/unitarian-universalist-beliefs-and-practices-701571.

[28] For more on Rastafarianism, see Edmonds, Ennis B. 2012. *Rastafari: A Very Short Introduction*. Oxford: Oxford University Press. See also https://www.learnreligions.com/rastafari-95695.

[29] Some diaspora religions trace back to African tribalism, while others are new innovations loosely based on tribal or other religions. Some African diaspora religions can also interface with Christianity or other larger existing traditions. For more on African diaspora religions, see Janzen, John M. 2017. "African Religion and Healing in the Atlantic Diaspora." Oxford Research Encyclopedias: African History. https://oxfordre.com/africanhistory/view/ 10.1093/acrefore/9780190277734.001.0001/acrefore-9780190277734-e-54

Cynthia: Alden, haven't you also had some experience in interfaith relations?

Alden: Yes, I have long worked with people of other faith traditions and organized various presentations allowing for multiple religious perspectives to be shared. It's interesting to me that some people fear looking outside their religious tradition. Maybe they're worried that they might leave their own behind? My experience has been quite the opposite. The more I learn about other religious beliefs, the more commonality and value I see in my own. I have come to believe all religions have something to teach us. So, I'm actually eager and excited to explore the beliefs of other traditions. I'm always learning something new from that.

Cynthia: How did you get interested in such a wide variety of beliefs?

Alden: Part of this came from my religious mission. Living in the Caribbean islands (specifically Martinique, Guadeloupe, and St. Martin) for two years, I encountered a wide variety of people with a vast variety of beliefs. You want just about any belief there is out there, I found it. Not only various Christian sects and denominations such as Catholics, Baptists, Pentecostals, Seventh-day Adventists, Jehovah's Witnesses, and the like, but I also met Rastafarians, spiritual mediums, spiritualists, Vodou practitioners, faith healers, Hindus, Jews, Baha'i, and of course agnostics and atheists. We had a Baha'i friend in particular on Guadeloupe who had organized a youth softball league, and my fellow missionaries and I volunteered to help with that every Saturday afternoon for several months. Working with him was my first extended interfaith collaboration experience, and I quickly grew to love it.

The one major religious group I actually don't remember interacting with much there in the Caribbean was Muslims. My first serious religious discussion with a Muslim came more than a decade after I returned, when I was married and in graduate school at the University of Iowa. That day, I learned I'd not only long been mistaken in some respects about Islam, but saw a lot of intriguing interfaith parallels between Islam and what I already believed. There were religious commonalities with traditional Christianity and Judaism as well. But in all those discussions—and especially with my Muslim friend—my eyes were opened to the fact that all these different believers were humans and well worth respecting. I also saw we had more commonalities than differences. Interfaith efforts and religious literacy have since been among my lifetime passions, and I love learning how much we all have in common.

* The views we express in these conversations are our own as private citizens and are not meant to represent the perspectives or policies of any other person, social group, or institution, including those of the religious organizations we attend or of our employer.

---

[30] For more on Wicca, neopaganism, and "New Age" religion and philosophy, see Doyle White, Ethan. 2016. *Wicca: History, Belief, and Community in Modern Pagan Witchcraft*. Brighton: Sussex Academic Press.

[31] For more on Zoroastrianism, see WorldAtlas. https://www.worldatlas.com/articles/top-countries-of-the-world-by-zoroastrian-population.html

We have seen that religion is widespread throughout the world in a variety of beliefs and creeds. Sometimes religious believers get the impression that their religious teachings are unique to their faith tradition, or that they are the only ones in the world who believe a given principle or doctrine. This is not necessarily so. In fact, many of the world's religions—especially the major world religions listed in the preceding tables—share several important core ideas and beliefs. Comparative religion scholars and religious observers alike have identified several of these.

For instance, as mentioned in the previous chapter, "The Golden Rule" is actually rather widespread. According to the Interfaith Network for the UK, teachings such as "do unto others as you would have others do unto you," or its variant, "love thy neighbor as thyself"—are far from unique to the Bible (see Matthew 7:12 and 22:39, for instance) or even Christianity. Variations of this encouragement to love and treat others as well as one's self exist in Judaism, Islam, Sikhism, Baha'i, Buddhism, and Jainism. As one example of The Golden Rule restated, the Interfaith Network gives the Jain Pratikraman Sutra (35:49)—which Dr. Martin Luther King, Jr. would later echo—as: "I forgive all beings; may all beings forgive me. I have friendship towards all, malice towards none" (https://www.interfaithweek.org/uploads/connect-web.pdf).

In another instance of commonality, the idea that religious believers should actively assist others who are in need, often called "charity," is expressed in many different religions around the world. According to Darlene Levy of Purdue University, this is not only common to Buddhism, Christianity, and Judaism, but constitutes *zakat*, one of the "Five Pillars" (basic beliefs and practices) of Islam. *Zakat* has a profound meaning in Arabic, giving the sense of cleansing or purifying as well as growing and increasing. So, *zakat*—required of all Muslims—is intended not only to relieve poverty but to help the giver improve and become purified. Some Muslims also give *sadaqah*, or additional voluntary charitable aid. Other religions across the world encourage giving aid to the less fortunate as well (https://www.purdueglobal.edu/blog/social-behavioral-sciences/helping-those-in-need/).

Likewise, Linda Groff and Paul Smoker in the *International Journal of Peace Studies* identify peace as a common theme in many different religions worldwide, citing specific examples from Sikhism, Islam, Hinduism, Christianity, Judaism, and even the noted sage Black Elk of the Lakota Sioux:

> *"Peace ... comes within the souls of men when they realize their relationship, their openness, with the universe and all its powers and when they realize that at the center of the universe dwells Wakan-Tanka, and that this center is really everywhere, it is within each of us"* (https://www.gmu.edu/programs/icar/ijps/vol1_1/smoker.html).

Various observers have also noted common religious themes and ideas between major religious groups. For instance, the Swiss theologian and Catholic priest Hans Küng (2004) identified a set of common religious principles as part of his larger Global Ethics initiative. The Markkula Center for Applied Ethics at Santa Clara University summarizes Küng's common values this way:

- Every human being must be treated humanely;

- Treat others as you like to be treated;

- Have respect for life; no violence;

Dignity, love, and the fair treatment of others are at the core of most religions across the globe.

- Deal honestly and fairly; no cheating, favoritism;

- Respect and love one another; cherish and love.

(https://www.scu.edu/ethics/focus-areas/business-ethics/resources/in-search-of-a-global-ethic/.)

Moreover, in a Huffington Post article entitled "*Reclaiming the Sacred: Five Uniting Religious Principles*" (2014), Maha Elgenaidi, founder and chief executive officer of the Islamic Networks Group, lists five common principles that she finds in Buddhism, Christianity, Hinduism, Islam, and Judaism:

1. **Respect for life**: Human life is not expendable, threats to it must be condemned, and provisions should be made for supporting it.

2. **Respect for dignity**: These religions teach an opposition to discrimination as well as respect for and the inherent worth of all humans.

3. **Respect for freedom of religion and conscience**: They advocate freely choosing a relationship with God or the sacred without force or interference.

4. **Respect for freedom of thought and expression**: This follows from respect for human life and dignity and includes the defense of civil liberties.

5. **Respect for others**: This is the ethic of reciprocity, also commonly known in America as The Golden Rule.

To conclude, in the words of Maha Elgenaidi (2014), "All religion thus sets as a primary aim the excellence of human character, the development of human beings who from the depth of their selves manifest kindness, compassion, truthfulness, courage, and all the virtues associated with the best of humanity." Religious groups despite their known flaws feature a great many principles that encourage their adherents to seek for the best in themselves and each other.

Of course, these common principles are found in non-religious people, too. The idea of implicit religion suggests that such values and ideals would be found in many social contexts, not just religion (Bailey 2011). However, these principles clearly indicate that believers in various religions worldwide have long been taught—for at least the last 4,000 years of documented history of Abrahamic religion—the importance of loving others as themselves, helping others, human worth, seeking peace, and so forth. Despite the obvious drawbacks of religion as we've known it—most notably the well-documented trouble many of these adherents have had actually putting these principles into practice! —the presence and influence of these common principles in most cultures worldwide speaks well of the long-term influence of religion within society.

CHAPTER 5

RELIGIOUS FAITH AS A MOTIVATOR FOR SOCIAL CHANGE IN ORGANIZATIONS

There is no fundamental social change by being simply of individual and interpersonal actions. You have to have organizations and institutions that make a fundamental difference.

—*Cornel West[1]*

We will now turn to discussion of religious faith as a motivator of social change on the level of social institutions and large organizations. As we do this, keep in mind that, as previously acknowledged, social change is not only for the better. It can also be for the worse. Religious faith has historically been used as a platform and rationale for violent social change. Whether discussing Roman expansion, the Crusades, the Inquisition, European colonialism, American westward expansion, Nazi aggression, or more recent religious extremist terrorism, religious faith was an important part of the propaganda used to solidify support for war and violence. In fact, the enemy population was commonly dehumanized and viewed as pagan or heretical.[2] Fortunately, religious faith has also been a very effective motivator for less violent social change, if not social change for the better. We will consider primarily this dimension in the following chapter as we consider how the "why" selects the "who."

Agents of social change are organizations, groups of individuals, and individuals that take action specifically to cause social change. What is meant by "organizations"? These are what sociologists call "social organizations." These include, for example, clubs, professional organizations, the military and veterans' organizations, consumer organizations, political parties, universities and alumni associations, hospitals, businesses, charitable organizations, recreation leagues, labor unions, and religious institutions. Of course, not all social organizations are religious institutions, nor are all

---

[1] Cornel West is an American educator, philosopher, and social activist. This quote and others can be found at: https://www.brainyquote.com/quotes/cornel_west_777699?src=t_social_change.

[2] Multiple scholars, analysts, and informed observers have cited dehumanization as a frequent strategy employed by those who seek to target large groups of individuals, encourage strife and warfare, and ultimately overthrow civil society in the name of authoritarianism. See Anolik, Ruth Bienstock and Howard, Douglas L., 2004 as well as http://www.museumoftolerance.com/education/teacher-resources/holocaust-resources/antisemitism-a-historical-survey.html and http://nationalhumanitiescenter.org/tserve/nineteen/nkeyinfo/mandestiny.htm.

Organizations can include a wide variety of special interests, such as clubs, professional organizations, universities and alumni associations, hospitals, businesses, charitable organizations, recreation leagues, and religious institutions. The people who are actively involved in these organizations may take action for social change because of their own deeply held religious beliefs.

social organizations agents of social change. Many are designed to simply facilitate everyday life, including work and leisure. However, many social organizations are effective agents of social change, particularly charitable organizations.

As Cornel West noted at the top of the chapter, organizations are vital in bringing about social change. A little later in the chapter, we will examine several organizations that participate in social change. Before examining these organizations, however, it's important to explore the context in which they exist and their overt purpose, which can be connected to religious reasons. These do not stem directly from actual religious groups—we do not have religious leaders secretly issuing directives to these organizations!—but they come indirectly from the influence of religion in culture as a whole. Remember the religious authorities mentioned in Chapter 4, such as Küng (2004) and Levy (2012), who identified some ideas that are common to most of the world's major religious groups. As we saw as part of that discussion, Maha Elgenaidi (2014) listed five common religious principles that are found in most of the world's major religions. We have chosen to repeat her words here and elsewhere, since they express these shared interreligious ideas very well and essentially restate those also identified by the other experts:

1. **Respect for life**: Human life is not expendable, threats to it must be condemned, and provisions should be made for supporting it.

2. **Respect for dignity**: These religions teach an opposition to discrimination and support respect for and inherent worth of all humans.

3. **Respect for freedom of religion and conscience**: They advocate freely choosing a relationship with God or the sacred without force or interference.

4. **Respect for freedom of thought and expression**: This follows from respect for human life and dignity and including the defense of civil liberties.

5. **Respect for others**: This is the ethic of reciprocity, also commonly known in America as The Golden Rule.

These pro-respect principles do not exist only in religious groups. Far from it. Instead, many religious groups have influenced the values, morals, and ideals found in larger society—and the values, morals, and ideals have in turn at times influenced religion as well. Most societies have laws about various aspects of public health and social order that range from directives about public safety (speeding and other traffic laws, non-smoking, etc.) to property law (vandalism, theft, etc.) to violent crime (rape, assault, murder, etc.). Many of these are also echoed in various forms of religious law, such as the Judeo-Christian Ten Commandments. In any case, religion can influence the creation of civil law in terms of the aspects Elgenaidi mentions, which is one way the "why" influences the "who" of social change.

For instance, note some laws that we sometimes laugh about today, several of which have been overtly influenced by religious concerns. For instance, blasphemy is still technically forbidden by law in Michigan,[3] and swearing at players or officials at sporting events for people older than 16 is illegal under Massachusetts state law.[4] (More on these and other peculiar state laws at https://www.mentalfloss.com/article/50041/50-weird-laws-still-books.) As an overall category, "blue laws" that prohibit various Sunday activities are frequently the subject of scoffing today, though they are increasingly rare, and where they are still on the books they are often unknown and rarely enforced. But the existence of laws of this kind are a testament to the influence of religion on the legal system, particularly in the eighteenth and nineteenth centuries in the early years of America (https://law.jrank.org/pages/4795/Blue-Laws.html).

On a more serious note, consider the Missouri 1830s "Mormon Wars" that culminated in a controversial gubernatorial order in 1838 that allowed settlers to use potentially lethal force to expel "Mormons" from the state. Most of that embattled religious group soon left under duress, effectively ending the conflict, and the order then lay forgotten for more than a century—meaning that it was legally defensible to assault or kill a member of that religious faith in Missouri until the order was rescinded in 1976.[5] In any case, religious concerns often indirectly influence laws, but sometimes can directly influence the legal code as well. The legal system is a key context within which the respect

---

[3] As of August 2020, the law against blasphemy in Michigan was still on the books. See the Michigan Compiled Laws, Section 750.102. http://www.legislature.mi.gov/(S(pknfcq2oj4b5apgskbjtgfqc))/mileg.aspx?page=getObject&objectName=mcl-750-102&highlight=750.102

[4] As of August 2020, using profane or obscene language against participants or officials at sporting events was punishable by a fine in Massachusetts. See Massachusetts General Laws, Section 36a. https://malegislature.gov/Laws/GeneralLaws/PartIV/TitleI/Chapter272/Section36a

[5] Missouri Gov. Lilburn Boggs issued the infamous "Extermination Order" in 1838 at the height of conflict between LDS and non-LDS settlers in several northwestern Missouri counties, tacitly allowing the use of potentially deadly force to expel the members of The Church of Jesus Christ of Latter-day Saints from the state. No known cases beyond the mid-19th century are on record of anyone in Missouri attempting to justify violent crimes according to this order. However, recognizing the outdated order's inhumanity and presumed unconstitutionality, a later governor of Missouri, Christopher Bond, officially rescinded it in 1976. For more information on these orders, see https://www.sos.mo.gov/archives/resources/findingaids/miscMormonRecords/eo.

for others mentioned by Elgenaidi is often enacted—or not enacted, as the case sometimes is—and influences the culture that inspires social change as well as the people who may well see the need for it. The "why" motivates the "who."

This interlinked context may be even more evident as we consider the concept of "civil religion," as noted by the venerable sociologist Robert Bellah (1967). More recent scholars such as Philip Gorski (2017) and Peter Gardella (2014) have since expanded on Bellah's framework. The essential idea, according to Bellah, is that the approach of American society and government to the country functions very much like a religion. Not only are there "sacred" national symbols such as the flag, but also music (National Anthem, God Bless America), saints (Washington, Jefferson, Lincoln), holy writings that determine national belief and practice (Declaration of Independence, Constitution), holy days (Fourth of July), revered sites (throughout Washington, DC and elsewhere), ritual oaths of devotion (Pledge of Allegiance), and many other aspects of national observance that directly resemble religious attitudes and behavior.[6]

Also notably, Bellah's concept of civil religion is often noted as one aspect of Bailey's framework of implicit religion (2011), in which various other elements of society also act very much like religion. Sports fans, for instance, follow their teams with a particular fervor that may resemble religious devotion. Some fans of popular culture such as Star Trek, Star Wars, Harry Potter, Lord of the Rings, The Chronicles of Narnia, and others display a quasi-religious devotion. Aspects of education, politics, military and paramilitary interests, and other social spheres seem to have religious aspects. Ironically, medical science and many scientific fields can also behave similarly, taking a certain amount of information "on faith" until they can establish what they can confirm as probable truth.

In any case, despite our modern attempts to separate church and state, the two are profoundly interlinked. The relationship between religion and civil society may well run deeper than we ever suspected—which is not necessarily a bad thing if we are focused on the common principles of religion that focus on respect for each other in the respects Elgenaidi has outlined. Much as we have positive and necessary reasons for separating church and state, it is actually *good* for civil society if those dimensions of mutual respect deriving from common religious principles remain internalized in our secular culture. That internalized respect for life, dignity, freedom of conscience, freedom of thought, and other people in our culture helps inspire and drive positive social change—especially when individuals see the lack of respect and wish to restore it.

Recalling our discussion of functionalism and social change from earlier in the book, in classical functional thought, the institutions and organizations among us help meet social needs. When we as a society have our social needs met, we aren't really all that concerned about social change. However, as the later critics of functionalism have noted for decades, when those social institutions become dysfunctional—that is, they have trouble meeting our social needs, or fail to meet them at all—dissatisfaction with the dysfunction sets in. This is also where the conflict perspective tends to emerge in social change, as well as the evolution as people debate and try to enact solutions, though this is getting a little ahead of ourselves. In dysfunctional terms, the dysfunction is recognized on the institutional level and the need for social change becomes evident.

---

[6] Civil religion should not be confused with nationalism, which is beyond Bellah's conceptualization. Nationalism can be seen as civil religion taken to the extreme. Instead of attitudes and behaviors about a country merely resembling religion, in nationalism those attitudes and behaviors actually become a form of religion in its own right. Nationalism goes beyond patriotism, or love of country, to what some would label actual worship of country. For more on civil religion, see https://www.mtsu.edu/first-amendment/article/1519/civil-religion.

Like a strong stone cathedral, religion as an institution may tend to be resistant to social change as much as it may promote it.

That being said, religion's role in institutional and organizational social change may actually be rather mixed. Why is that? We see that throughout history, religion as an institution has often been powerful enough to act in its own interests, or perhaps that of the most powerful individuals who have been directing it. So on the institutional level, its overall influence as a driver of social change may actually be counterbalanced if not cancelled out with an impulse to preserve the status quo. Likewise, in line with Weber's classic discussion of the institutional difference between the prophet who innovates within the organization and the priest who strives to preserve it (Berger 1963), institutional religion tends to innovate and preserve alike. These observations may partly explain why we do not more often see religion included as one of the foremost drivers of social change on an institutional and organizational level.

To further explain how this applies to religion on the institutional level, also consider the concept of church-sect typology, which has a rather interesting history itself.[7] In short, church-sect typology postulates that there are several different types of religious organizations. The most notable are **churches**, which exist in a state of low tension with the outside world since they are more inclined to accommodate themselves to the state of society; **sects**, which exist in a state of high tension with the

---

[7] Church-sect typology, sometimes referred to as "church-sect theory," has passed through a great many theorists' hands and rather than becoming more refined and streamlined, seems to have developed additional complications depending on the scholar working with it. Hence we use the "typology" designation here. The concept started with Max Weber, whose student Ernst Troeltsch reformulated it, and additional religious scholars such as J. Milton Yinger, Benton Johnson, H. Richard Niebuhr, William Swatos, Roland Robertson, and yet others have lent their ideas to striving to refine the concept. See http://hirr.hartsem.edu/ency/cstheory.htm. We are borrowing largely from Johnson's tension model of church-sect typology, as well as a more recent discussion from David Bromley and Gordon Melton. See their article "Reconceptualizing Types of Religious Organizations" in *Nova Religio: The Journal of Alternative and Emergent Religions*, vol. 15, no. 3, pp. 4-28.

outside world and generally "push back" against the state of society; **denominations**, which exist in varying states of tension with each other and the outside world; and **cults**, or in some formulations of the typology, the broader term **New Religious Movements**, which are often in high tension with the outside world, like small sects. Here, too, is Weber's prophet-priest tension.

The key component in terms of social change is the relationship of the religious organization to the outside world. This formulation of church-sect typology would suggest that relatively little institutional motivation for social change would originate from religious groups that would be considered churches since they exist in relatively low tension with the outside world and would be expected to seek to accommodate. On the other hand, a high degree of institutional motivation for social change could conceivably originate with sects and their tension with the outside world, and still more motivation with denominations or "cults"—or perhaps better said, New Religious Movements.

Though our upcoming case studies cannot confirm this, since they are operating on a different level of analysis, the question of if—and how—sects or churches, as well as denominations and New Religious Movements, might contribute to social change is intriguing. In any case, the concept of church-sect typology suggests that different institutions might approach social change somewhat differently, with low-tension religious organizations more inclined to favor the status quo and their higher-tension counterparts advocating for more substantial change. If this idea holds up, it could possibly help account for the mixed influence of religion on social change at the institutional level, since some organizations might uphold the status quo while others would strive to change it, presumably according to what would yield the most benefit.

With these ideas in hand, let's turn to a discussion of how the common religious principles as well as the religious ideals that have permeated our society manifest themselves in a set of organizations that participate in social change. In 2016, Forbes (Barrett, William) compiled a list of the top ten US

© Mino Surkala/Shutterstock.com

Many religious organizations have their own relief institutions, such as the Seventh-day Adventists' Development and Relief Agency.

charitable organizations based on total contributions. Many of these charitable organizations have principles that can be traced back to religious concerns (noted in italics by the author) as part of their written mission statements:

1. **United Way Worldwide**, $3.708 billion

   "Our Mission: United Way improves lives by mobilizing the *caring power of communities around the world to advance the common good*. We all have a stake in what befalls our fellow man. We all benefit when a child succeeds in school, when someone finds a job that will help them provide for their family, or when more people are able to access quality, affordable health care. We rise or fall together" (http://unitedwayworldwide.org).

2. **Task Force for Global Health**, $3.154 billion

   "Our Work: Our program areas include *neglected tropical diseases, pandemic preparedness, polio eradication, field epidemiology training, public health informatics, and health workforce development*. Neglected tropical diseases (NTDs) are burdens for many developing countries. These diseases cause blindness, disfigurement, cognitive impairment, stunted growth, and even death. We implement comprehensive programs to control and eliminate five NTDs – blinding trachoma, river blindness, lymphatic filariasis (elephantiasis), intestinal worms, and schistosomiasis. The world is increasing vulnerable to pandemics of influenza and other infectious diseases. The Task Force is working with low- and middle-income countries to strengthen the systems necessary to immunize their populations quickly against these diseases. The Task Force is also playing critical roles in the 'last mile' of polio eradication. Our work to strengthen health systems also focuses on training frontline health workers in how to detect and respond to disease outbreaks such as Ebola and by improving the use of information to protect and promote health. We also help developing countries build human resource information systems to manage the licensing requirements of their healthcare workforce" (https://www.taskforce.org).

3. **Feeding America**, $2.150 billion

   "Working together to *end hunger*: The Feeding America network is the nation's largest domestic hunger-relief organization. Together with individuals, charities, businesses and government we can end hunger. In a country that wastes billions of pounds of food each year, it's almost shocking that anyone in America goes hungry. Yet every day, there are millions of children and adults who do not get the meals they need to thrive. We work to get nourishing food – from farmers, manufacturers, and retailers – to people in need. At the same time, we also seek to help the people we serve build a path to a brighter, food-secure future" (http://www.feedingamerica.org/hunger-in-america).

4. **Salvation Army**, $1.904 billion

   "The Salvation Army, an international movement, is an evangelical part of the universal Christian Church. *Its message is based on the Bible*. Its ministry is motivated by the love of God. Its mission is to preach the gospel of Jesus Christ and to *meet human needs* in His name *without discrimination*. Doing the most good: FIRST, we assess the needs of each community in which we serve. We work to understand the obstacles, hardships, and challenges native to the area's particular population. NEXT, we build local programs designed to offer immediate relief, short-term care, and long-term growth in the areas that will best benefit the community. THEN, we offer the local programs to the local community, working to continually optimize their efficacy via spiritual, physical, and emotional service" (https://www.salvationarmyusa.org/usn).

The Salvation Army's red bucket donation drive is a visible part of the Christmas season, especially in large American cities.

5. **YMCA of the USA**, $1.202 billion

"Our cause defines us: We know that lasting personal and social change comes about when we all work together. That's why at the Y, *strengthening community* is our cause. Every day, we work side-by-side with our neighbors to make sure that *everyone, regardless of age, income or background*, has the *opportunity to learn, grow and thrive*" (http://www.ymca.net).

6. **St. Jude Children's Research Hospital**, $1.181 billion

"*Finding cures. Saving children.* The mission of St. Jude Children's Research Hospital is to advance cures, and means of prevention, for pediatric catastrophic diseases through research and treatment. Consistent with the vision of our founder Danny Thomas, *no child is denied treatment based on race, religion or a family's ability to pay*" (https://www.stjude.org).

7. **Food for the Poor**, $1.156 billion

"*Saving lives… transforming communities… renewing hope*: We do our best to *meet needs both physical and spiritual*, as well as at the individual, family and community level. We *provide food, housing, emergency relief and much more to those in desperate need.* We feel a special calling and are uniquely equipped to serve the poorest of the poor in the Caribbean and Latin America" (http://www.foodforthepoor.org).

8. **Boys & Girls Club of America**, $923 million

"Our mission: To enable all young people, especially those who need us most, to reach their full potential as *productive, caring, responsible* citizens. Our vision: Provide a world-class Club Experience that *assures success is within reach of every young person* who enters our doors, with all members on track to graduate from high school with a plan for the future, demonstrating *good character* and citizenship, and *living a healthy lifestyle*" (https://www.bgca.org).

9. **Catholic Charities USA**, $921 million

"The mission of Catholic Charities is to *provide service to people in need*, to advocate for *justice in social structures*, and to call the entire church and other people of good will to do the same. As Catholic Charities, we labor in the streets *inviting and serving* those who have been left out to know and *experience the tremendous and abundant love of God through Jesus Christ*. We commit ourselves to break down walls of division that keep sisters and brothers separated from one another, excluded, or rendered disposable by our society. With joy, we resolve to *build bridges of hope, mercy and justice* toward the creation of a culture of communal care responsive to the cries of those who are poor" (https://www.catholiccharitiesusa.org).

10. **Goodwill Industries International**, $902 million

"Goodwill works to *enhance the dignity and quality of life of individuals and families* by strengthening communities, eliminating barriers to opportunity, and helping people in need reach their full potential through learning and the power of work" (http://www.goodwill.org).

In 2016, CNBC (Caminiti, Susan) compiled a list of the top 10 international charities based on budgets and net assets (dollar figures were not listed by CNBC. CNBC recommended that all donors do their research by checking the charity's ranking based on financial health, accountability, and transparency as listed by Charity Navigator[8], Charity Watch[9], and/or BBB Wise Giving Alliance[10]). CNBC's 2016 (Caminiti, Susan) list included:

1. **Direct Relief**

"Healthy people. Better world. Direct Relief is a humanitarian aid organization, active in all 50 states and more than 80 countries, with a mission to *improve the health and lives of people affected by poverty or emergencies – without regard to politics, religion, or ability to pay*. Direct Relief's assistance programs are tailored to the particular circumstances and needs of the world's most vulnerable and at-risk populations. This tradition of direct and targeted assistance, provided in a manner that respects and involves the people served, has been a hallmark of the organization since its founding in 1948 by refugee war immigrants to the US" (https://www.directrelief.org).

---

[8] Charity Navigator is an organization that evaluates charitable organizations based on financial health and accountability. You can learn more about Charity Navigator, plus your favorite charities, by going to their website at https://www.charitynavigator.org.

[9] Charity Watch considers itself to be "America's most independent, assertive charity watchdog." They evaluate charitable organizations based on financial reports and then rate the charity based on the percentage of total expenses spent on programs and based on how much it costs the charity to bring in $100 of cash donations from the public. You can learn more about Charity Watch and find the ratings for charities at their website: https://www.charitywatch.org.

[10] BBB Wise Giving Alliance accredits charities as meeting the BBB's Charity Standards by evaluating 20 different accountability issues. You can view their list of accountability issues for each charitable organization by visiting their website at http://www.give.org/.

2. MAP International

"MAP International is a *Christian organization providing life-changing medicines and health supplies to people in need. MAP serves all people, regardless of religion, gender, race, nationality, or ethnic background.* We provide medicines and health supplies to those in need around the world so they might experience life to the fullest. In times of disaster, MAP International provides immediate *humanitarian assistance and relief aid* including medicines and health supplies to people left homeless and without access to basic services. From the earliest days of a response, MAP focuses on helping communities restore critical services and work with partners to help them rebuild health systems" (https://www.map.org).

3. The Rotary Foundation

"Rotary is a global network of 1.2 million neighbors, friends, leaders, and problem-solvers who see a world where people unite and take action to create lasting change – across the globe, in our communities, and in ourselves. Solving real problems takes real commitment and vision. For more than 110 years, Rotary's people of action have used their passion, energy, and intelligence to take action on sustainable projects. *From literacy and peace to water and health, we are always working to better our world,* and we stay committed to the end" (https://www.rotary.org).

4. Samaritan's Purse

"*Samaritan's Purse is a nondenominational evangelical Christian organization providing spiritual and physical aid to hurting people around the world. Since 1970, Samaritan's Purse has helped meet needs of people who are victims of war, poverty, natural disasters, disease, and famine with the purpose of sharing God's love through His Son, Jesus Christ. The organization serves the church worldwide to promote the Gospel of the Lord Jesus Christ.* After sharing the story of the Good Samaritan, Jesus said 'Go and do likewise.' That is the mission of Samaritan's Purse—to follow the example of Christ by helping those in need and proclaiming the hope of the Gospel" (https://www.samaritanspurse.org).

Samaritan's Purse set up emergency respiratory care units in tents in New York City's Central Park during the COVID-19 pandemic in the spring of 2020.

5. **AmeriCares**

"Health is on the way. Every day, somewhere in the world, *our neighbors face hurricanes, floods, disease outbreaks, civil conflict, earthquakes, extreme poverty and other crises. Their need for health care* has never been greater. For people affected by poverty or disaster, health is essential to a better future. With good health, they can *attend school, be productive at work, care for their families and contribute to strong communities.* Poor health puts all of those opportunities at risk. Health is fundamental to all aspects of development. Our donors and partners help our health programs, medicines and supplies reach our neighbors in need in more than 90 countries and all 50 states in the US each year" (https://www.americares.org).

6. **Catholic Medical Mission Board**

"We believe in a world in which *every human life is valued, and health and human dignity are shared by all. Inspired by the example of Jesus,* CMMB works in partnership globally to deliver locally sustainable, quality health solutions to women, children, and their communities. Despite the progress in global health, women and children living in developing countries continue to be among the most *vulnerable.* This motivates us to focus on improving their lives and the lives of their communities" (https://cmmb.org).

7. **Billy Graham Evangelical Association**

"Founded by Billy Graham in 1950, BGEA exists to *proclaim the Gospel of Jesus Christ by every effective means* and to equip the church and others to do the same. The Billy Graham Rapid Response Team *trains God's people for grief ministry and deploys crisis-trained chaplains to provide emotional and spiritual care to those affected by man-made or natural disasters*" (https://billygraham.org).

8. **Caring Voice Coalition**

"Caring Voice Coalition is dedicated to *improving the lives of patients with chronic illnesses.* We accomplish our mission by offering empowering, supportive and comprehensive outreach services. Caring Voice Coalition was founded in 2003 to support people with rare diseases who often had no place to turn in the face of soaring medical costs. CVC provides insurance and disability education and counseling, as well as *aid programs* for insured or underinsured patients. With this distinct, holistic approach, CVC programs *empower and support* patients and their families, as well as the friends who care for them." (See healthwebnav.org for more information about CVC.)[11]

9. **United Nations Foundation**

"The United Nations Foundation links the UN's work with others around the world, mobilizing the energy and expertise of business and non-governmental organizations to help the UN tackle *issues including climate change, global health, peace and security, women's empowerment, poverty eradication, energy access,* and US-UN relations. The United Nations Foundation is honored to work with you and the United Nations to *foster a more peaceful, prosperous and just world*" (http://www.unfoundation.org).

---

[11] As the publication deadline for this book approached, it became clear that the COVID-19 pandemic and other factors have substantially affected the mission and operations of the Caring Voice Coalition. We have kept CVC for reference as an example of an organization that nonetheless reflects religious motivation and concerns, but acknowledge that they may not be currently operating normally, if at all.

10. Natural Defense Council

"The Natural Resource Defense Council *works to safeguard the earth – its people, its plants and animals, and the natural systems* on which all life depends. Since 1970, NRDC has worked to ensure the rights of all people to clean air, clean water, and *healthy communities.* We combine the expertise of nearly 500 scientists, lawyers, and advocates with the power of more than two million activists to confront our planet's most pressing problems" (https://www.nrdc.org).

In all twenty charitable organizations listed above, Maha Elgenaidi's (2014) first religious principle (respect for life) and second religious principle (respect for dignity) are mentioned as part of their mission statement or in their listed work, whether implied or stated implicitly (noted in italics above by the author). Respect for others is also frequently referenced or implied throughout these organizations' mission statements. While some organizations do not specify any religious faith, others in the list, clearly state their religious affiliations and beliefs. Such principles and values are often integrated into the larger culture due to the influence of religion, whether directly or indirectly. Despite the tendency of some religious organizations to meet the status quo, others appear motivated on the institutional level to meet the unmet needs clearly present in the world.

It, therefore, appears that even though religion strives to change and preserve alike on the institutional level, religious faith is an active motivator of social change for many humanitarian organizations. Some openly state so, while others are simply influenced by those values, ideas, and principles expressed in the larger culture. In this way, social change happens, with the institutions and large groups being necessary for widespread and lasting alteration, as indicated by Cornel West at the top of the chapter. Working through institutions and organizations is necessary for the "who" to accomplish the "why"—and the "what"—of social change.

Notes from the Authors*

Cynthia: Alden, interesting thoughts on social institutions and religion. In your class, don't you go a bit more into the history of how religion helped shape society long ago?

Alden: Oh, certainly. Yes, the link between religion and culture is more historically profound than most people realize. For instance, the entire layout and division of the Western Hemisphere as we know it goes back to the 1493 *Inter Caetera* Papal Bull of Pope Alexander VI following the Columbus voyage. The Catholic church was then so powerful that Alexander's ecclesiastical decree was accepted as politically legitimate. Alexander—formerly a wealthy Spanish Castilian, Rodrigo Borgia, friendly to fellow Castilians King Ferdinand and Queen Isabella—essentially granted Spain colonization rights to the vast majority of present-day North and South America. He also granted Spain's rival Portugal a small slice of the tip of far eastern South America—where modern-day Recife, Brazil is located—and the colonization rights to Africa. Big surprise—Portugal wasn't satisfied! The Portuguese negotiated an adjusted settlement in the 1494 Treaty of Tordesillas, which slightly expanded Portugal's New World territory. The Portuguese eventually expanded their South American territory well beyond Tordesillas, establishing Brazil and some territory in Africa. Spain later ceded most of North America to England and France, keeping much of their Central and South American territory much longer. Still, the *Inter Caetera* decree set the initial parameters of the Western Hemisphere. If religion played a key role in literally shaping the geography and culture of the Western world, of course it also helped bring about other forms of social change.

(Continued)

Cynthia: What about the separation of church and state? You indicate there isn't as much as most people believe.

Alden: Oh, there certainly isn't. Just to make sure I'm clear about this, it is definitely better to try to separate church and state than not to try at all. Neither should gain an undue influence on the other. Ever. The separation of church and state is important, especially given that the First Amendment forbids government from restricting religion, and Thomas Jefferson's "wall of separation" doctrine has been legal precedent nearly since America's beginning. All sorts of awful outcomes have happened throughout history when either religion or government has become powerful enough to suppress the other. So we need to at least try separation.

That said, if you consider the idea of implicit religion, as well as the deeper implications of civil religion, church and state actually can't ever be fully and completely separated. Absolute separation of church and state just isn't socially or logically possible. The best we can hope for is to keep each from controlling the other or gaining an unfair advantage. It's like a pickup basketball game between powerful and skilled but sometimes clumsy opponents. Both sides—religion and government—are going to commit fouls as they play. That just happens. But the two sides have to take it upon themselves and their mutual honor to call each other's fouls, ensure a clean game, make sure neither side is favored, and maintain order. It's tricky because, aside from the people watching the game happen (we the people!) there aren't any other third-party referees who can ensure these outcomes. But we have to try our best.

Cynthia: We continue to see a decline in public trust of our social institutions. What do you think about that, and what does it mean for social change?

Alden: This is one of the most concerning aspects of modern society. When we as a society don't trust our religious leaders, doctors, journalists, scholars, government, other countries, or even our own neighbors, who do we trust? We have seen that all come home to roost, as it were, in the COVID-19 pandemic of 2020. We have qualified medical doctors telling us what to do to combat the coronavirus and minimize its influence. Countries like New Zealand have actually responded well to this pandemic with masking, social distancing, strict yet humane border control, a temporary lockdown for the sake of long-term public health, and so forth. Yet in America, with some of the world's most qualified epidemiologists and other experts advocating similar measures, all the best advice in the world gets shot down the second some sensationalistic video pops up on YouTube by someone somewhere claiming some degree of medical knowledge declaring this virus a hoax or complaining about wearing masks in the name of freedom. This has been highly aggravating to my physician and other medical-field friends who are actually trying to treat people who have become sick with this very real virus. But this is what happens when the public at large stops trusting social institutions.

True as it is that various individuals within each of our historical social institutions have at times been mistaken—which will happen, even in scientific fields as testing and triangulation takes place!—or even at times deceptive, this doesn't warrant the widespread pushback against the institutions themselves. The social change resulting from widespread institutional distrust is most definitely not change for the better. We as a society need to be wiser about how we react to expert opinion. The experts may not always be right about everything, but the cost of rejecting them wholesale far outweighs any rewards.

* The views we express in these conversations are our own as private citizens and are not meant to represent the perspectives or policies of any other person, social group, or institution, including those of the religious organizations we attend or of our employer.

CHAPTER 6

RELIGIOUS FAITH AS A MOTIVATOR FOR SOCIAL CHANGE IN GROUPS OF INDIVIDUALS

Little people doing little things in little places everywhere can change the world.

—Anwar Fazal[1]

As we move forward with discussing how the "why" influences the "who" in terms of religion and social change, we will now move to a different level of analysis. In Chapter 5, we discussed religion and social change on the institutional and organizational level. There, we defined **agents of social change as those organizations, groups of individuals, and individuals that take action specifically to cause social change,** and we discussed organizations making social change. However, even though organizations are vital for lasting social change to occur, we are left to examine where the motivation comes from. What about groups of individuals? Is religious faith and its common principles a motivator for social change in the hearts and minds of groups of people? "Societies remain stable because enough people define existing conditions as satisfactory and they [the societies] change because enough people define the once accepted conditions as problems that must be solved" (Newman 2011).

In the past few years, several groups of people, not accepting the existing conditions as satisfactory, have formed new social movements in efforts to make changes to society. **Social movements are groups of people who share a common concern and have an agreed-upon agenda for social change.** "Movement participants seek to draw attention to their cause, change public opinion, and force those in authority to address their grievances" (Massey 2016). But why do they do this? What motivates people to launch social movements, and what role does religion play in launching such movements? We will explore that in this chapter, discovering why, in the words of Anwar Fazal above, the "little

---

[1] Anwar Fazal is a civil society activist in Malaysia, focusing on consumer advocacy, health issues, the environment, sustainability, and peace. In addition, Mr. Fazal was awarded the 1982 Laureate by The Right Livelihood Foundation. This quote can be found at https://www.wiseoldsayings.com/social-change-quotes/#ixzz6U7XSz9ju. Additional information including a biography, video, and quotes can be found at https://www.rightlivelihoodaward.org/laureates/anwar-fazal/.

People with a vision of what should be can do huge things to make change.

people"—by which he obviously meant ordinary individuals, or at least individuals who appear to be ordinary before they decide to engage social change—are motivated to speak out and act to make a difference in the world.

In Chapter 5, we discussed functionalism as a theory of social change. That theory, which considers how organizations and institutions meet social needs and work towards equilibrium—and also how organizations and institutions may fall short of doing so—seems to fit that level of analysis well. Here in this chapter, as we explore how religion and social change relates to groups and individuals, we will explore a little more in terms of functionalism, expand on the conflict and evolutionary perspectives of social change, and integrate a religious explanation of why social change may occur on those levels. Since groups and individuals are often interlinked, we will discuss how both work in depth in this chapter, and simply recap in Chapter 7.

Throughout this book, we have been asking this recurring question: How does the "why" select the "who" in terms of social change? As we examine how this question applies to groups and individuals, note first of all that we shift a little away from the functional perspective of social change more towards the views of conflict and evolutionary development. This is not to say that functionalism doesn't have its place in this discussion—it does—but it is to say that conflict and evolutionary development have a more significant role. In our last chapter, we mentioned that in the earliest formulations of functional theory, institutions and organizations were thought to meet social needs and reach equilibrium. However, later theorists noted that dysfunction and disorder are also not only possible, but nearly inevitable. As institutions strive to meet social needs, tension arises. Groups and individuals exist and operate more often in an environment of conflict and evolution, which also produces social change.

At this point, it may be useful to introduce the basic idea of the Hegelian dialectic. Credited to the German philosopher Georg Wilhelm Friedrich Hegel (Maybee 2019), the essential framework is this: One idea or *thesis* encounters an opposing idea or *antithesis*, and the result is worked out in a *synthesis.*[2] Hegel believed this essential pattern explained a wide variety of phenomena from religion to history itself, and social change would certainly be included in this. The assumption is that social change is generally for the better, which is not necessarily the case.

The idealistic Hegel failed to consider this at much length, but another German idealist who later came across Hegel's ideas did not. This philosopher, more inclined to seek out "how things work in the real world," saw Hegel's dialectic as too abstract and ethereal, considered instead how it applied to what he could see around him, and decided to reformulate the Hegelian dialectic for the here-and-now in real life in the material world. His name, of course, was Karl Marx. So, when Marx (1996) wrote in the *Communist Manifesto* that all history was the history of class struggle, he was in part directly challenging Hegel and his dialectic. As the poor proletariat (thesis) interacts with the wealthy bourgeoisie (antithesis), the result is not some neat, tidy resolution—as Hegel's synthesis would be, of course—but an ongoing struggle that is only resolved when the proletariat can manage to throw off the oppression that's been imposed. This has been the core tenet of Marxist conflict theory since its nineteenth century origin.

Still, as also mentioned in a previous chapter, Marx was not exactly a fan of religion. So, the field of religious studies, including the sociology of religion, draws relatively little from Marxist analysis. Relatively few religious people find much sympathy with Marxist thought as well. Consequently, we would not expect at the outset to find a great deal of sympathy for Marxism among activists who engage in social change for religious reasons. Yet the larger concerns of class, power, social stratification, poverty, and oppression remain significant for Marxists and religious believers alike. We would simply expect that those concerned with these fields from a religious standpoint would engage the issue of conflict from a different standpoint than the Marxists would. This remains a curious subject for further analysis in examining how the "why" selects the "who" of social change when looking at the issue from a conflict standpoint and raises several interesting questions. How do religious people approach this issue and conceptualize the conflict as those groups and individuals work to bring about social change? How does the conflict they see and perceive motivate them to work for change? Might themes such as a sense of good and evil, what's right and wrong, or events and circumstances being "ordained by God" play further roles in the social change they seek to bring about?

Also significant, in terms of group and individual approaches, is the evolutionary perspective of social change—simply explained, the idea that social change will create a better world. This idea is reflected in the Anwar Fazal quote at the top of the chapter. As he expressed it, ordinary people in ordinary places doing ordinary things can and do create tremendous change. This is a more Hegelian outlook, of course, in terms of optimism that the world is changing for the better due to groups and people striving to change it. But this may be the rationale many individuals who are motivated by religious concerns feel most comfortable aligning with. The difference that they feel inclined to work towards, and the purpose they feel they want to have happen, can only help the world become a better place as a result. The world can evolve into a better place due to their work, which is a concern shared by many involved in the religious world.

---

[2] The Hegelian dialectic has actually been a prevalent historical pattern in much of Western philosophy, but is often credited to Georg Wilhelm Friedrich Hegel because he explained it in depth and wrote extensively about it. One relatively concise yet excellent explanation of the Hegelian dialectic is given at https://lucian.uchicago.edu/blogs/mediatheory/keywords/dialectic/; Julie Maybee gives a more in-depth treatment at https://plato.stanford.edu/entries/hegel-dialectics/. Marx's critique also took note of Hegel's corollary to the dialectic in terms of history, which Hegel designated the "zeitgeist," or "spirit of the times." So when Marx wrote in the Communist Manifesto that all history had been the history of class struggle, this was part of his very literal reformulation of Hegel's dialectic in material rather than abstract terms.

Here again, we wish to bring up our previous discussions about common religious principles, as in Elgenaidi (2014) and others who have identified values and ideas that are prevalent in many religious contexts across the world. As mentioned in previous chapters, Elgenaidi finds that a respect for human life, the value of others, worth and dignity, freedom of religion and conscience, and thought and expression are all common to most religions across the world. These shared principles and ideas—a sort of "brotherhood of humanity"[3]—are the lifeblood of those motivated by religion to engage in social change. The "what" that drives the "who" to create social change in the modern context is rarely religious evangelism *per se* for any particular church or religious faith.

© ItzaVU/Shutterstock.com

The Stone of Hope at the site of the Martin Luther King Jr. Memorial in Washington, DC, depicts Dr. King looking forward. This subtly recalls his famous "I Have a Dream" speech, given near that site on August 28, 1963, containing the significant line: "With this faith… we will be able to hew out of the mountain of despair a stone of hope." See the entire speech at https://kinginstitute.stanford.edu/king-papers/documents/i-have-dream-address-delivered-march-washington-jobs-and-freedom.

That said, we did see evangelization to Christianity underlying the push to colonize the Western Hemisphere and much of Africa and Asia from the fifteenth to eighteenth centuries. However, it seems difficult in that case—which occurred on the nation-state level anyway rather than the group and individual levels—to disentangle those religious aims from a political and primarily secular eagerness to acquire the rich natural resources available in those areas. So, let's note that we are speaking directly of religious concerns in the abstract as a primary motivating factor for groups and individuals.

Nearly all religious-motivated activists come from their own particular religious backgrounds and perspectives, of course. However, they are less worried about persuading others to join their particular faith traditions than they are about ensuring that they work together well with other like-minded individuals despite whatever differences may exist in their religious perspectives. They build upon common religious ground rather than focus on distinctions and divergences. This interfaith impulse encourages building bridges rather than walls between different groups of people in society.

Remember, also, with the broader perspective that the concept of "implicit religion" yields (Bailey 2011), the motivation for groups and individuals to engage in social change can go well beyond overtly religious ideas, concerns, and directives. Activists may engage in social change not necessarily because they believe

God has called them to do so, but also because they feel it's the right thing to do from a moral or ethical standpoint. They may feel a sense of identification with or admiration for Mother Teresa, Mahatma Gandhi, or yet others, seeing them as heroes and role models in their own right. They may feel a sense of duty or fairness because they have learned what they have learned or been given the resources they've been given. It's actually possible to create an argument that all activism is implicitly religious in that sense, though since this issue and project lies beyond the scope of this book, we will stop short of it and simply make the note of the possibility.

Where does the impulse to act in accordance with religious values and concerns originate? One answer is religious socialization, which can be distinctly thought to contribute to social change. As socialization occurs within a particular group, a person learns to become part of that group. The individual comes to understand not only the ideas, thoughts, values, and attitudes that the group values and expects, but also the legacy, traditions, actions, and behaviors the group wants to see in one that claims membership in it. Through socialization, the individual learns to become part of the group. This is an initial process, with a learning curve for someone who has just joined the group, as well as a lifelong component (Sherkat 2003, Guest 2011).

As individuals are socialized into a group, they adopt a particular worldview that the group helps create for them. Individuals build their own lifeworlds, to be sure, but in line with a self-assembly kit metaphor, the essential parts of the worldview are supplied by the group along with assembly instructions. However, notably, individuals still bring their own personalities and perspectives, along with previous life experiences, and they build the worldview through not only the socialization of the group but also with the aid of their own backgrounds. The resulting socialization and worldview definitely creates a context within which individuals come to see the world in particular ways (Sherkat 2003). This can include a perceived need—the "what"—along with a desire to change that world according to the perceived lack, or the "why," which would most definitely inspire the "who."

This brings to mind our previous discussion of the distinction Max Weber made between the priest and the prophet (Berger 1963). In brief, relating back to the original institutional structure, the priest will seek to maintain and preserve it, while the prophet will introduce innovations within that structure, trying to make changes and improvements. This applies not only to the structure itself, but to the behavior of individuals within it—hence the prophets' frequent calls for change and repentance (*Ibid.*). The prophet's role is to encourage social and institutional change, a role that could be influenced by socialization, adoption of worldview, or the individual's past background alike. Akin to church-sect typology on the institutional level, the prophet exists in a state of tension with the outside environment that ostensibly requires change. Tension arises, and the prophetic individual responds to the tension by advocating for change and pushing back against the tension. The tension with outside society combined with a prophetic role and worldview could possibly be another factor motivating the "who" in terms of individual-level social change.

Another factor related to socialization is the possibility of media—particularly media that endorses social change. Media is a prevalent factor throughout religious settings, as old as hymns and religious art and iconography. Narratives and legends are pervasive throughout religion, including heroic tales of past religious figures and role models, or even cautionary tales. These can acquire the power of legend, as Joseph Campbell has pointed out, thereby giving the media narrative or symbol mythological power (1988), which may also have a mystical element. Mythology can also contribute to the appeal of the media narrative or symbol on the level of religion, or at least relatively close to it.

As with the rest of society, most activists learn about other activists through media of some sort—a book (even one like this!), movie, TV, website, social media site, and so forth. Particular individuals may be inspired by identifying with a certain activist through media, one common strategy of media appeal (Cohen 2011), or accounts of a particular activist may resonate mythologically with particular individuals, who may see the activist as a type of hero or role model (Campbell 1988). The possibility of media involvement in group and individual activism alike is well worth further study, particularly with the possibility of mythological resonance adding to the appeal of the media narrative or symbol.

Even more directly than mythological resonance, some religion-inspired activists may well feel intended, inspired, or even directed by deity to engage in social change due to an actual religious experience. For example, though arguably exceptional, one of the historical individuals we name in Chapter 7 as an interesting case in point of religion-inspired social change is Joan of Arc. By her own account and those of others as well, she felt that she had been called by the angels she spoke with and the Catholic Christian God to lead the French armies in 1429, thereby saving her country from British conquest (BYUtv 2015).

Hers was a particularly dramatic religious experience, but it's much more common for individuals to have religious experiences on a more subtle level, after which they may feel the need to engage in social change. Dr. Martin Luther King was a particularly eloquent and educated pastor, though he never claimed to have been personally directed by God to lead the Civil Rights movement, and certainly not at all in the sense Joan of Arc led French troops. However, he did claim to be following God's will in doing so in several speeches and certainly served as a classic case in point of Weber's conceptualization of a prophet.

Most of Dr. King's language was symbolic or alluded to Biblical imagery and even a religious experience—though his described religious experience was generally of a symbolic rather than a literal type. He clearly had a vision for civil rights, but generally described his own vision as his personal hopes and desires rather than any sort of religious vision or angelic communication in the Joan of Arc sense. Still, he often alluded to the religious experiences of others to underscore the power of his own vision. This became particularly poignant in the last public speech he ever gave on April 3, 1968, in which he not only invoked a parallel with the Old Testament's Moses but seemed to foreshadow his imminent demise:

> … I don't know what will happen now. We've got some difficult days ahead. But it doesn't matter with me now. Because I've been to the mountaintop. And I don't mind. Like anybody, I would like to live a long life. Longevity has its place. But I'm not concerned about that now. I just want to do God's will. And He's allowed me to go up to the mountain. And I've looked over. And I've seen the promised land. I may not get there with you. But I want you to know tonight, that we, as a people, will get to the promised land. And I'm happy, tonight. I'm not worried about anything. I'm not fearing any man. Mine eyes have seen the glory of the coming of the Lord.[4]

---

[4] The paragraph cited is the conclusion of "I've Been to the Mountaintop," Dr. King's last public speech, given April 3, 1968, to the striking city sanitation workers at Memphis' (Tennessee) Mason Temple. The next day, he was assassinated at the Lorraine Hotel in Memphis. See the full text of the speech at https://www.afscme.org/about/history/mlk/mountaintop.

In any case, Dr. King was prophetic, whether in the foretelling or the Weberian sense. He and many others worked for social change, being directly motivated by religious concerns for the betterment of others and society in general. Socialization and adoption of a particular worldview may well be crucial concepts in accounting for how religion helps motivate social change. Many individual activists have found they are able to accomplish what they did—or what they have—because they are part of a larger group that backs them up and helps them coordinate their efforts. The group also helps them turn their worldview into reality.

Changing gears slightly to more applied settings, let's take a look at several social groups and movements that are active today in the United States. Many of these groups/movements have religious principles as part of their written mission statements. As in Chapter 4's discussion of common religious principles, we have italicized ideas that resemble the religious principles echoed in these groups' mission statements, particularly those that resonate with Elgenaidi (2014) and the discussion of respect for these common-religious principles: **Respect for life, respect for dignity, respect for freedom of religion and conscience, respect for freedom of thought and expression, and respect for others.**

These social groups/movements include:

- **Black Lives Matter**

  "#BlackLivesMatter was founded in 2013 in response to the acquittal of Trayvon Martin's murderer. Black Lives Matter Foundation, Inc is a global organization in the US, UK, and Canada, whose mission is to eradicate white supremacy and *build local power to intervene in violence inflicted on Black communities by the state and vigilantes.* By combating and countering acts of violence, creating space for Black imagination and innovation, and centering Black joy, we are winning immediate *improvements in our lives.* **We are expansive.** We are a collective of liberators who believe in an inclusive and spacious movement. We also believe that in order to win and bring as many people with us along the way, we must move beyond the narrow nationalism that is all too prevalent in Black communities. We must ensure we are building a movement that brings all of us to the front. We *affirm the lives* of Black queer and trans folks, disabled folks, undocumented folks, folks with records, women, and all Black lives along the gender spectrum. Our network centers those who have been marginalized within Black liberation movements. **We are working** for a world where Black *lives are no longer systematically targeted for demise.* **We affirm our humanity,** our contributions to this society, and our resilience in the face of deadly oppression. The call for Black lives to matter is a rallying cry for ALL Black lives *striving for liberation*" (https://blacklivesmatter.com/about/).

- **March For Our Lives**

  "Our Mission: To harness the power of young people across the country to fight for sensible gun violence prevention policies that *save lives.* Our Story: Not one more. In the days after the tragedy at Marjory Stoneman Douglas High School in Parkland, Florida, we knew we had to make sure that what happened to our community never happens again. We cannot allow one more person to be killed by senseless gun violence. We cannot allow one more person to experience the pain of losing a loved one. We cannot allow one more family to wait for a call or text that never comes. We cannot allow the normalization of gun violence to continue. We must create a *safe and compassionate nation* for all of us" (https://marchforourlives.com/mission-story/).

- **Me Too**

   "In 2017, the #metoo hashtag went viral and woke up the world to the magnitude of the problem of sexual violence. What had begun as local grassroots work had now become a global movement—seemingly overnight. Within a six-month span, our message reached a global community of survivors. Suddenly, there were millions of people from all walks of life saying "me too." And they needed our help. Today, our work continues to focus on assisting a growing spectrum of survivors—young people, queer, trans, the disabled, Black women and girls, and all communities of color. We're here to help each individual find the right point of entry for their unique healing journey. But we're also galvanizing a broad base of survivors, and working to *disrupt the systems that allow sexual violence* to proliferate in our world. This includes insisting upon accountability on the part of perpetrators, along with the implementation of strategies to sustain long term, systemic change. So that one day, nobody ever has to say "me too" again (https://metoomvmt.org/get-to-know-us/histoty-inception).

- **TIME'S UP**

   "*Safe, fair, and dignified* work for women of all kinds. We insist upon a world where everyone is safe and respected at work. A world where women have an equal shot at success and security. A world where no one lives in fear of sexual harassment or assault. By helping change culture, companies, and laws, TIME'S UP Now aims to create a society *free of gender-based discrimination* in the workplace and beyond. We want every person—across race, ethnicity, religion, sexuality, gender identity, and income level—to be safe on the job and have equal opportunity for economic success and security" (https://www.timesupnow.com/about/).

Marchers for the #MeToo and #TIMESUP movements march in front of San Francisco City Hall on January 20, 2018 to protest sexual harassment and advocate for safe working environments for women.

Historically, the United States has experienced a wide variety of social movements, but since many are no longer well-organized, it is difficult to assess their motivating factors. However, some of the historic movements appear to have had religious principles as part of their efforts. Let's take a look at a few:

- **Anti-Nuclear Movement**

  An international movement that was particularly active during the 1960s, 1970s, and 1980s, resisting the development and use of nuclear power and nuclear weapons.[5] *This movement showed concern for human life.*

- **Anti-War Movement**

  In the United States, this was the anti-Vietnam War movement of the 1960s and 1970s.[6] Anti-war movements typically occur when a nation is preparing for an armed conflict, and yet, a vocal portion of the citizenry do not support the war. *This movement showed concern for human life.*

- **Chicano Movement & Farm Workers Movement**

  Both movements occurred alongside the American civil rights movement during the 1940s, 1950s, and 1960s. They demanded reforms in Hispanic American civil rights, citizenship, voting rights, education, and farm labor conditions. The United Farm Workers union is still very active in working for the rights of America's farm workers.[7] *This movement showed concern for human life and dignity.*

- **Civil Rights Movement**

  The American civil rights movement was very active during the 1950s and 1960s, pushing for equality, voting rights, education, and justice for African Americans. The NAACP continues to fight for federal advocacy, education, economic opportunity, criminal justice, health, and environmental/climate justice.[8] *This movement continues to work for human life and dignity.*

- **Disability Rights Movement**

  The disabilities rights movement occurred in large part as a consequence of many World War II veterans returning home to America from war with significant disabilities. The movement gained momentum alongside the American civil rights movement during the 1960s. They

---

[5] The anti-nuclear movement is often treated as two separate movements: anti-nuclear power and anti-nuclear weapons. For more information about the anti-nuclear power movement, multiple articles can be accessed at the Global Non-violent Action Database's website: https://nvdatabase.swarthmore.edu/category/wave-campaigns/anti-nuclear-power-movement-1960s-1980s. For more information about the anti-nuclear weapons movement, consider reading: Harvey, Kyle. *American Anti-Nuclear Activism, 1975-1990: The Challenge of Peace.* 2014.

[6] The Vietnam War was a painful time in American history where the war and those fighting the war were not supported by a large portion of the American population. Much of the social unrest of what is known today as "The Sixties" (actually from about 1966-74) relates back to sentiment against the Vietnam War. For further information, go to https://www.ushistory.org/us/55d.asp.

[7] For more information and music recordings from the Chicano movement, go to the US Library of Congress website: https://www.loc.gov/item/ihas.200197398/. And for additional information on the farm workers movement, go to the United Farm Workers website at https://ufw.org/research/history/ufw-history/.

[8] For timelines, articles, and videos on the civil rights movement, go to https://www.history.com/topics/civil-rights-movement. The NAACP initiated its #WeAreDoneDying initiative in June 2020 after the death of George Floyd. For more information about the NAACP and its initiatives, visit your local chapter or go to https://www.naacp.org/.

The path for LGBTQ rights in America has been a long and socially difficult one with impassioned discussions about human dignity.

demanded civil rights for disabled people, which finally gained legal success with the passing of the Americans with Disabilities Act in 1990.[9] *This movement continues to work for human life and dignity.*

- **Gay Rights Movement & LGBTQ Social Movement**

  In 1969, the Stonewall Riots solidified the demands of the gay rights movement in the United States. The movement demanded civil rights for gay men initially, but eventually included all men and women of all sexualities.[10] *This movement continues to work for human dignity.*

- **Immigrants' Rights Movement**

  The Immigrants' Rights movement is an extension of the Chicano movement of the 1940s-60s. The movement demands civil rights and due process for all immigrants in America no matter their legal status, and is supported by a wide variety of organizations, including the National Immigration Law Center (https://www.nilc.org/), the American Civil Liberties Union (https://www.aclu.org/issues/immigrants-rights), and United We Dream (https://unitedwedream.org/).[11] *This movement continues to work for human life and dignity.*

---

[9] For additional information on the disabilities rights movement and the Americans with Disabilities Act, go to https://ability360.org/livability/advocacy-livability/history-disability-rights-ada/ and https://www.ada.gov/.

[10] For historic photos, biographies, and timelines of the gay rights movement, including the Stonewall Riots, go to https://www.history.com/topics/gay-rights/history-of-gay-rights. For more information on the LGBTQ social movement, consider reading Stulberg, Lisa M. *LGBTQ Social Movements.* 2018.

[11] For more information on the Immigrants' Rights movement in the United States, consider reading Nicholls, Walter J. *The Immigrant Rights Movement: The Battle Over National Citizenship.* 2019.

- **Indigenous Peoples Movement**

  The Indigenous Peoples movement occurred alongside the American civil rights movement during the 1950s, '60s, and '70s. They demanded civil rights for indigenous people, the return of stolen land, and repatriation of indigenous artifacts.[12] *This movement continues to work for human life and dignity, plus freedom of religion.*

- **Labor Movement**

  The Labor Movement in America finds its roots in the Industrial Revolution and the need to improve pay, benefits, and working conditions.[13] *This movement continues to work for human dignity.*

- **Mothers Against Drunk Drivers (MADD)**

  This movement began in 1980 with a group of grieving moms pushing for laws against drunk driving and preventative education.[14] *This movement continues to work for human life.*

- **Women's Rights & Feminist Movement**

  Both a national and international movement, the Women's Rights movement demands civil rights, voting rights, rights of property ownership/inheritance, and rights over their own bodies. Progress is widely varying depending on the country and religious group the woman is living within.[15] *This movement continues to work for human dignity and life, plus freedom of religion and speech.*

Religious faith and its principles, particularly Maha Elgenaidi's (2014) first religious principle (respect for life) and second religious principle (respect for dignity) appear to be represented in the work of these social movements (noted in italics above by the author). It therefore appears that religious faith was historically and is presently a motivator of social change for at least some groups of people in America. In the next chapter, we will discuss some individuals who have participated in social change for at least partly religious reasons.

---

[12] For articles, audio interviews, and videos on the historic and present days struggles of the Indigenous Peoples movement, go to https://indigenouspeoplesmovement.com/ and https://dp.la/primary-source-sets/the-american-indian-movement-1968-1978.

[13] For American labor timelines and additional information, go to the website of the American Federation of Labor and Congress of Industrial Organizations (AFL-CIO): https://aflcio.org/about-us/history.

[14] For additional information about the high cost of drunk and drugged driving and Mothers Against Drunk Driving, go to https://www.madd.org/.

[15] For information on the international struggle for women's rights, go to the United Nations website on women at https://www.unwomen.org/en, the Human Rights Watch website at https://www.hrw.org/topic/womens-rights, and Amnesty International's website https://www.amnesty.org/en/what-we-do/sexual-and-reproductive-rights/. For a historical perspective on women's rights in the United States, go to the National Women's History Alliance's website at https://nationalwomenshistoryalliance.org/history-of-the-womens-rights-movement/.

Cynthia: I'm interested in the idea of religious experience that we brought up. It's not always necessary for individuals to engage in social change, right? But haven't studies found that religious experiences make a difference in people who have them?

Alden: Oh, yes, definitely. Much of the literature on religious experience indicates that people who have such experiences have profound shifts in life perspective and behavior. Life becomes more meaningful, they gain a sense of purpose, they appreciate other people and relationships more than before, they are less afraid of death (particularly in the case of near-death experiences), and so forth. Michael Argyle (2009) provides a case in point, in which in addition to life perspective changes, he found that religious practices like prayer, events such as worship services, substances such as entheogenics, and even particular events like music or sunsets can help launch religious experiences. Occurrences like dreams and feelings like "being called" can also be interpreted as religious or spiritual experiences. The changes in perspective and life approach seem intriguing in terms of religion and social change, since such cognitive and emotional shifts might seem to parallel a desire to bring about social transformation.

Still, this is anything but a given for all of religion and activism. At this point, the link between actual religious experience and social change still seems too murky to infer anything other than that a desire to work towards making a difference could be one possible outcome of a religious experience. As with Joan of Arc, some individual activists over time clearly did feel that they were intended or "called" to do what they did, or at least like Dr. King were convinced that they were doing precisely what God wanted them to do. However, not all religious activists report such feelings or experiences.

Furthermore, as we noted, we could actually argue that all activism is inherently religious from an implicit-religion standpoint, though that opens up a whole new fresh can of worms, too. That whole new question goes into the heart of what activism is and why people engage in it, and to fully explore, it would require tearing down a lot of what we've already built up in this book as well as what others have done. It's a tantalizing possibility and question, but more of the implications need to be thought through before going forward. So it's best to note this issue as an intriguing question and save it for future research.

Cynthia: Sounds good! Socialization is really quite critical to social change and we mentioned media. Should we expand a bit more on the role of the media in social change?

Alden: Of course. Now, as I've been known to tell students, colleagues, Facebook friends, and others, "The Media" doesn't exist—at least not in the sense of some highly biased, secretly interlinked, shadowy unified conspiracy of corporations and communications organizations out to brainwash us all and conquer the world. That's only a social construct. We have corporate media in news and entertainment, true, but we also have citizen media and social media. We participate in the process, not just have it visited upon us. It's all biased—we don't escape that—and we just pick what we think we can trust.

(Continued)

That socializes us, too, whether or not we recognize it, and it's a process that's very familiar given religious dynamics. The curious tendency of social media is that the more we engage with others, the more we "dig in" on our own positions and the less we adapt to those of others. We've decided what we think and we're just finding our own "facts" to support our own viewpoints. Strangely, that's religious behavior. The resulting social change we're collectively bringing about on social media is polarization, as many people swing to one side or the other.

As we polarize, we ironically use media to criticize media, which as Peter Berger pointed out in *The Heretical Imperative* (1979) is a reductive religious strategy. But we also use media to support our own viewpoints—a deductive religious approach. Moreover, some of us are "seeking"—an inductive religious technique—to become more informed by searching for a variety of perspectives. This is the wisest course to follow if we really want to be informed. Our socialization should help us strive to seek learning and education via multiple sources and perspectives. In short, though "The Media" only exists as a social construct, media usage is inevitable, as is socialization. We simply should be careful which media sources we trust.

Cynthia: Oh, I agree with that, definitely. I'm really quite careful with the media I use. I know when my boys were younger, I was careful to find out about what books they were required to read in school. I wasn't ever one of the book-banning people—not at all—but I just wanted to make sure I knew what they were reading and be sure they were ready for the issues that arose in those books. There's nothing in those books that shouldn't ever be discussed at some point, but we make a mistake when we make children think about issues too early—before their minds have developed enough to process the issues abstractly, or before we've been able to teach them about how they should best think about those issues.

Alden: Yes. It's wise to be careful about the media we use. We can't avoid using media—it's part of the fabric of our everyday lives—but we can be careful about which media we trust. Media are a key part of social change, too. It's not mind control—we're not living in *1984*—but it is a matter of agenda-setting. To paraphrase Bernard Cohen (1963), media aren't nearly as successful at telling us what to think as they are at telling us what to think *about*.

For example, you probably don't remember the dramatic nationwide coverage of the August 10, 2020 derecho storm that devastated much of Cedar Rapids, Iowa, knocked out power for a couple of weeks for a couple of hundred thousand people, and ruined millions of dollars worth of crops—because the coverage didn't happen. Also, in the news cycle then: Joe Biden chose Kamala Harris as his running mate, Russia released a preliminary but widely heralded COVID-19 vaccine, and there was talk of cancelling the entire college fall sports season. The Iowa derecho wasn't ignored altogether, but it certainly took lower billing despite the potential for the damage to have more far-reaching implications than those other stories. In any case, media suggest what's important to society, and society then follows the priorities set by media.

Cynthia: Yes, our media certainly appear to set the agenda. In the summer of 2020, racial injustice in America was very much at the top of that agenda. You said earlier that you were interested in racial issues. What are your thoughts on Black Lives Matter? I've indicated what I think earlier in the book, but what's your take?

(Continued)

Alden: Wow, I'm glad you asked. Keeping in mind I'm Caucasian and have had a fair amount of privilege because of that, I can still try to relate. I'll never be a Black man in America or completely know what that's like. But I can be an ally of those who do. That said, I've seen a great deal of confusion about this group. So many people have been told BLM is some secret, shadowy organization trying to do all sorts of awful stuff. Still, we are discussing BLM here rather than Chapter 5 for a reason—BLM is best described as a movement of concerned people, not an official centralized organization. The closest thing to a nationwide "Black Lives Matter" organization in existence is a nonprofit 501c established in Delaware, which was established to make BLM donations tax-deductible. Sure, there's also a website to raise awareness, as we showed in our chapter. But there's no BLM CEO, governing board, mid-level managers, or anything of the sort.

Various groups in America call themselves "Black Lives Matter," plus this or that, and they're all led by different people and have slightly different objectives. They don't often coordinate their strategies. In fact, some different BLM groups were formed in some areas due to disagreements *about* strategies. So, when you hear nonsense being thrown around about some high-ranking official in Black Lives Matter somewhere who did something awful, sometimes that's misinformation talking. There is no single centralized BLM organization that commands and controls everything that happens in BLM's name. It's a social movement, and multiple groups are using the BLM phrase.

Protesters in New York City after the death of several African-American men in 2016.

So, we can't paint everyone from BLM with the same brush. Some people affiliated with some BLM groups have done horrible things. We're dealing with humans here, and humans do good and bad alike. Most BLM activists actually are peaceful, though a few BLM groups are more willing to resort to violence and confrontation than others. That's not a good idea, as I see it, but then again, as Dr. King once said, a riot is the language of the unheard (Rothman 2015). Black athletes have protested peacefully by taking a knee during the National Anthem for quite some time now. When people ignore these peaceful protests or belittle and insult the protesters for peacefully protesting, I'm not sure we as a society can justifiably complain when the protests stop being peaceful. We need to listen to what BLM has to say. Obviously, if all lives really and truly did matter, nobody would ever have to say, "Black Lives Matter." That's important to understand.

(Continued)

Cynthia: That's what I've noted in my interactions with friends and students as well. We need more people paying attention and helping to solve the problem of racial injustice and police brutality against minorities. All lives *should* matter, but it's fairly clear from what we see in the world around us today that not all lives actually *do* matter. Christianity teaches that God is love, right? As I see it, a loving God would want social justice for His children. That inspires me to do the work I do as well.

Alden: Yes, I agree. It's important to work for the difference we want to see. By the way, Cynthia, we've chatted a lot throughout the text, but as you know, the next chapter on individuals and social change is pretty intense, as are our case studies. Let's save our *Notes from the Authors* for the concluding chapter—especially since our case studies are pretty much our notes, with a lot of help from the activists we've interviewed.

Cynthia: That sounds fine! We'll share some more notes in our case studies and as we wrap up.

* The views we express in these conversations are our own as private citizens and are not meant to represent the perspectives or policies of any other person, social group, or institution, including those of the religious organizations we attend or of our employer.

7 RELIGIOUS FAITH AS A MOTIVATOR FOR SOCIAL CHANGE IN INDIVIDUALS

I am only one, but still I am one. I cannot do everything, but still I can do something and because I cannot do everything, I will not refuse to do the something that I can do.

—Edward Everett Hale[1]

As stated in Chapter 5, **agents of social change are those organizations, groups of individuals, and individuals that take action specifically to cause social change**. We discussed organizations in Chapter 5 and groups of individuals in Chapter 6. So, what about individuals? Are religious faith and principles motivators for social change in the hearts and minds of individuals?

Of course, the organizations and groups involved in making social change are made up of active individuals. Barack Obama stated in his first interview (Rhodan 2017) after leaving the office of President of the United States, "…ordinary people, when working together, can do extraordinary things." Most individuals work quietly behind the scenes, but a few become publicly visible leaders. Donald Trump stated in December 2014 (http://twitter.com/ realDonaldTrump) before becoming President of the United States, "In the end, you're measured not by how much you undertake but by what you finally accomplish."

As we discussed in Chapter 6, individuals who work for social change are acting in a prophetic role, in the terms of early sociologist Max Weber. Unlike the priests who preserve the status quo, the prophets innovate and make changes, and invite others to change as well (Berger 1963). Much of this is likely due to their socialization, religious and otherwise, as the worldview they have adopted (Sherkat 2003) helps them see new possibilities in the world, care about making a difference in it, desire to work for the good of others, and strive to follow through with actions on the impulses they feel in their hearts and minds. They often exist in a state of tension with the outside world, striving to

---

[1] Edward Everett Hale was a nineteenth and early twentieth century American Unitarian minister and author, credited with being part of the Social Gospel movement. His most famous work is possibly the short story, "The Man Without a Country." For a biography and information on Hale's "Lend a Hand Society," go to http://www.lend-a-hand-society. org/. Source of quote: https://www.forbes.com/quotes/author/edward-everett-hale/.

© Gri Nati/Shutterstock.com

meet the unmet needs they see and make changes to help others. They may be inspired by religious experience, though most in rather subtle ways, and they may have encountered examples of previous activists in the media they have encountered as part of their socialization. In this way, individuals work for social change due to religious concerns.

We can easily identify many individual agents of social change. In this chapter, we have identified many individuals throughout history who have acted as social change agents due to religious concerns, but have put together a list of 50 to identify and discuss in more detail. These 50 people made a substantial difference in the world with some degree of religious faith as their motivation or rationale for social change. The social change desired or brought about by these 50 individuals may or may not have produced what readers (or even we) consider to be positive social change, but either way, each of these individuals had a huge impact on society. Many of these individuals were leaders of armies, industry, art, science, philosophy and politics, and even religion. This is neither a comprehensive list, nor is it ranked. Rather, our list is more of a historical sampling to illustrate how religion has played a role throughout history in inspiring various individuals to engage in social change. We will further explore a handful of twentieth century religious social influencers following this list of 50.

This list of 50 leaves out other notable individuals. This includes not only several people quoted at the beginning of each of our chapters, but also some prominent religious leaders throughout history. For instance, we haven't included several significant Renaissance-era popes (Innocent VIII and successor Alexander VI, Leo X, Clement VII and successor Paul III) whose enduring legacy of social change was not exactly positive, or the more modern John XXIII and John Paul II, who oversaw more positive changes, as has current Pope Francis I.

Other notable unlisted religious figures include Ann Lee, Aimee Semple McPherson, Latter-day Saints (LDS) leaders Joseph Smith and Brigham Young, Native American (Shawnee) spiritualist leaders Tecumseh and his brother Tenskwatawa, noted theologian-authors such as Ralph Waldo Emerson, Edward Everett Hale (quoted above), and Clive Staples Lewis, writers such as Henry David Thoreau, Sir Arthur Conan Doyle (neither openly "religious" but both profoundly influenced by spiritual ideas) and staunch Catholic J.R.R. Tolkien, anti-poverty activists such as Jane Addams and Louisa Twining, and even US presidents Abraham Lincoln and John F. Kennedy. The role that religion and/or spiritual concerns played a role in the social change these individuals participated in should also not be left altogether unnoticed.

In any case, we are naming and spotlighting with footnotes these 50 individuals as historical cases in point of individuals who engaged in social change with religion as a prime motivator:

Andrew Carnegie.

- Abraham[2]
- Adolf Hitler[3]
- Alexander the Great[4]
- Andrew Carnegie[5]
- Baha'u'llah[6]
- Bob Marley[7]
- Buddha (Siddhartha Gautama)[8]

---

[2] Abraham is the patriarch of Judaism, Christianity, Islam, and Baha'i faiths. His story can be found in the Bible (Genesis 12-25). He is believed to be the father of the Hebrew people through his son Isaac and the father of the Arab people through his son Ishmael.

[3] Adolf Hitler was born in 1889, became Chancellor of Germany in 1933, and was the leader of Nazi Germany until his death in 1945 at the end of World War II. His policies led to the genocide of 6 million European Jews. For further information about Adolph Hitler, see https://www.biography.com/dictator/adolf-hitler. For a detailed discussion on Hitler's religious beliefs, read Richard Weikart's *Hitler's Religion: The Twisted Beliefs That Drove the Third Reich*.

[4] Alexander the Great was born in 365 BC, a son of King Philip II of Macedonia. He believed himself to be a descendant of the gods with a divine purpose and said he was often directed through dreams. Alexander, through military conquest of Persia, unified an empire from Greece to Egypt (to the south) and Pakistan (to the east). For more information on Alexander the Great, go to https://www.livescience.com/39997-alexander-the-great.html.

[5] Andrew Carnegie was a wealthy American businessman, best known for the Carnegie Steel Company in Pittsburgh, PA, which he sold for $480 million in 1901. Carnegie not only became a generous philanthropist as part of his Presbyterian (Protestant Christian) belief system, but argued that God expected the rich to "give back" to society in his 1889 booklet *The Gospel of Wealth*. He declared, "The man that dies thus rich dies in disgrace." For more information, see https://www.history.com/topics/19th-century/andrew-carnegie and https://www.carnegie.org/about/our-history/gospelofwealth/.

[6] Baha'u'llah was born in Tehran, Iran in 1817 and is believed by those of the Baha'i religious faith to be the most recent "Manifestation of God" on earth. For a photographic narrative of Baha'u'llah's life, go to https://www.bahaullah.org/.

[7] Born in 1945 and passing away in 1981, Bob Marley was a Jamaican reggae singer-songwriter. He was a devout Rastafarian and was seen by his fellow Jamaicans as a poet and a prophet. To learn more about Bob Marley's music, desire for social change, and life, go to https://www.bobmarley.com/ and https://www.rollingstone.com/music/music-news/the-life-and-times-of-bob-marley-78392/.

[8] Buddhism is based on the teachings of The Buddha, born Siddhartha Gautama. He lived as a wandering holy man in ancient Nepal and India approximately 2500 years ago. For photos, historical biography, teachings, and practices, see https://thebuddhistcentre.com/buddhism.

- Carry Nation[9]
- Caesar Augustus (Octavian)[10]
- Cesar Chavez[11]
- Charlemagne[12]
- Charles Martel[13]
- Confucius[14]
- Constantine the Great[15]

© Lucian Milasan/Shutterstock.com

Bob Marley (anonymous artist).

---

[9] Carry Nation (sometimes spelled "Carrie") was a famously radical member of the Women's Temperance Movement in Kansas. She was arrested for smashing a saloon with a hatchet in 1900, for which she is remembered in modern folklore. Carry believed that she was "on a mission from God" to remove the social ill of alcoholism. To learn more about Carry Nation and her mission, go to https://www.smithsonianmag.com/smart-news/three-things-know-about-radical-prohibitionist-carry-nation-180967627/ and https://www.alcoholproblemsandsolutions.org/carry-nation-biography-carrie-nation/.

[10] Born in 63 BC, Caesar Augustus was Julius Caesar's great-nephew and heir to his throne, as well as Egypt's first Roman emperor after defeating Cleopatra and Mark Anthony's armies. Augustus' political savvy and laws initiated a 200-year span of peace for Rome and his empire spanned from Britain to India. After his death, the Roman Senate declared him a god. For more information about Caesar Augustus, see https://www.nationalgeographic.com/culture/people/reference/augustus-caesar/.

[11] Cesar Chavez was an American, Roman Catholic, farm labor and Latino civil rights leader who grew up in the Great Depression as a migrant farm worker. He organized the Farm Workers Movement and the National Farm Workers Association, which eventually became United Farm Workers of America (UFW). For Cesar's speeches, writings, views, photos, and biography, go to https://chavezfoundation.org/.

[12] Uniting most of Europe in the middle ages, Charlemagne was Emperor of the Holy Roman Empire from 800 until his death in 814 CE. Charlemagne is considered to be the father of modern Europe, engaging in educational reform and church/monastery construction, plus encouraging prosperity through agricultural advancements. For additional information, go to https://www.ancient.eu/Charlemagne/.

[13] Charles Martel ("martel" means "hammer" in French) was the military ruler of the Frankish kingdom (modern-day France and Germany) and believed that a professional army rather than conscripts were necessary to defend his empire against non-Christian armies. In the Battle of Tours in 732 C.E., Charles' professional army defeated the Umayyad Muslim invaders, pushing them south of France and restricting their domain to Andalucia in southern Spain. For a timeline, images, and biography, go to https://www.heritage-history.com/index.php?c=resources&s=char-dir&f=martel.

[14] The father of Confucianism, Confucius was a Chinese philosopher about 500 BC who taught the need for love of humanity, worship of ancestors, respect for elders, self-discipline, and conformity to rituals. Confucianism remains a significant philosophy in China to this day. For videos, art, and biography, go to https://www.biography.com/scholar/confucius.

[15] Constantine the Great (Constantine I) was born in 272 AD and was the first Roman emperor to convert to Christianity. In 311 AD, Constantine's army crushed a rival army to win control of Rome. Constantine's army carried banners with the Greek letters Chi-Rho, corresponding to XP, meaning Christ. Constantine moved the center of Roman government to his newly named city, Constantinople (formerly Byzantium, today Istanbul), in 324 AD. Constantine encouraged the consolidation and standardization of the Christian belief system through the Nicene Creed (325 AD), which is still used throughout Christianity today. For a detailed illustrated biography, see https://www.historyextra.com/period/roman/constantine-great-life-facts-christian-roman-emperor-europe/.

- Cyrus the Great[16]
- Galileo[17]
- Genghis Khan[18]
- George Washington[19]
- Gregor Mendel[20]
- Harriet Beecher Stowe[21]
- Harriet Tubman[22]
- Helen Keller[23]

© Everett Collection/Shutterstock.com

Galileo (anonymous artist).

---

[16] Cyrus the Great united most of the Middle East under his Persian rule, thus founding the Achaemenid Empire in the sixth century BC. Considered one of the most benevolent conquerors in history, Cyrus the Great (Cyrus II) allowed his subjects to practice their cultures and religions without interference. Cyrus worshipped a variety of Iranian gods and is commonly thought to be a Zoroastrian, though some dispute this. For photos, maps, and a biography, go to https://www.ancient.eu/Cyrus_the_Great/ and https://www.nationalgeographic.com/culture/people/reference/cyrus-the-great/.

[17] Galileo Galilei, a Catholic Italian astronomer and scientist in the 1600s, improved the telescope and discovered the moons of Jupiter. Even more, like Nicolaus Copernicus a hundred years before, Galileo's scientific observations went against the religious, scientific, and political belief that the earth was the center of the universe. Church authorities put Galileo under house arrest for heresy in 1633. For additional information, including videos on Galileo's life and discoveries, go to https://www.smithsonianmag.com/science-nature/Galileos-Revolutionary-Vision-Helped-Usher-In-Modern-Astronomy-34545274/ and https://www.space.com/15589-galileo-galilei.html.

[18] Genghis Khan was the founder of the Mongol Empire in the twelfth century. His empire stretched across Asia into the Middle East, and included military attacks in eastern Europe and as far as present-day Ukraine. He believed that Daoist priests knew the secret to eternal life. For photos, maps and a biography, see https://www.livescience.com/43260-genghis-khan.html and https://www.ancient.eu/Genghis_Khan/.

[19] Known as the Father of the United States, George Washington was the Commander in Chief of the Continental Army during the Revolutionary War and took office as the first President of the United States in 1789. President Washington worked to ensure religious freedom within the United States. For additional information, including photos, quotes, and a detailed discussion of Washington's religious beliefs, go to https://www.whitehouse.gov/about-the-white-house/presidents/george-washington/ and https://www.mountvernon.org/george-washington/.

[20] Known as the Father of Genetics, Gregor Mendel was a Catholic Augustinian monk in Moravia whose research in creating hybrid varieties of peas led to basic understanding of hereditary traits and genetics. For additional information on genetics and Mendel's research, see https://www.nature.com/scitable/topicpage/gregor-mendel-a-private-scientist-6618227/.

[21] Harriet Beecher Stowe was an American abolitionist and author during the 1800s. Her most famous work was *Uncle Tom's Cabin* in 1852, though she published more than 30 books. For photos, quotes, biography, and additional writings, go to https://www.harrietbeecherstowecenter.org/.

[22] Known as "Moses" to her people, Harriet Tubman was an African American escaped slave who helped more than 300 people escape Southern slavery as a conductor of the Underground Railroad. Harriet had visions and dreams that she believed were from God. She was a devout Methodist. Harriet also served as a soldier, scout, nurse, and spy for the Union Army during the Civil War. In 1896, Harriet founded the Harriet Tubman Home for the Aged. For photos and a biography, go to https://www.britannica.com/biography/Harriet-Tubman.

[23] Helen Keller became both blind and deaf in 1881 at age 19 months as a result of an unknown illness. As an adult, she became a world-wide celebrity and worked for the American Foundation for the Blind (AFB) where she was a strong and visible advocate for the blind. Helen Keller, as a Protestant influenced by Emmanuel Swedenborg, wrote *My Religion* in 1927. For an extensive biography, see https://www.afb.org/about-afb/history/helen-keller/biography-and-chronology/biography. Helen's story was depicted in the film *The Miracle Worker* (1962). To see Helen's legacy and continued work, go to https://www.hki.org/helen-kellers-life-and-legacy/.

- Homer[24]
- Jesus Christ[25]
- Joan of Arc [26]
- Johann Sabastian Bach[27]
- John Adams[28]
- John Calvin[29]
- John Newton[30]
- Julius Caesar[31]

Joan of Arc (anonymous, stained glass).

© Nancy Bauer/Shutterstock.com

---

[24] Believed to have been the author of *The Iliad* and *The Odyssey*, Homer is widely recognized as the earliest and most important Greek writer. Tradition has it that Homer was a blind wanderer in Greece between the years 750-700 BCE. Homer was undoubtedly a believer in the Greek gods as highlighted in his epic poetry. For Homer's poetry and biography, see https://www.ancient-literature.com/greece_homer.html.

[25] Jesus Christ (Jesus of Nazareth) was a wandering first-century Jewish leader who founded Christianity. In the New Testament (Matthew, Mark, Luke, and John), Jesus declares himself to be the Messiah, "The Anointed One," who was to be the fulfillment of the covenant of God with Israel, though Judaism does not agree with this claim. Islam declares Jesus to be a prophet of God. Christianity declares Jesus to be the "Son of God," a member of the Holy Trinity of God, and the "Sacrificial Lamb of God." Jesus' teaching included the love of God and the love of your neighbor (Mark 12:28-31; Matthew 22:35-40 and Luke 10:25-28). Christians believe that Jesus' death and resurrection fulfilled prophecies of the Old Testament, particularly those of Isaiah (Isaiah 52:7 and Isaiah 61:1-2). For further details on Jesus' life, spoken words, prophecies about Jesus, and various religious beliefs about him, go to https://www.ancient.eu/Jesus_Christ/ and The Holy Bible.

[26] A peasant girl who said she spoke with angels and had visions from God, Joan of Arc became a military leader of France at age 17 in 1429, winning victory against the invading English army at Orléans and several others. She was captured a year later by the English and was eventually burned at the stake as a heretic. Joan of Arc was canonized by the Catholic Church and is the patron saint of France. For additional information and video documentary, go to https://www.biography.com/military-figure/joan-of-arc and https://www.byutv.org/player/98102eb7-69d9-45e5-9322-2e9d7284c3a6/joan-of-arc-joan-of-arc?listid=103cf34d-352e-4c43-a964-01ca2846f816&listindex=0

[27] Johann Sebastian Bach, born to a court trumpeter in 1685, is considered to be among the greatest composers of Western music. Bach spent most of his life composing, playing the organ, and directing music for the Lutheran Church in Leipzig, Germany. See more biographical information at http://www.baroquemusic.org/biojsbach.html; see http://www.classical.net/music/comp.lst/bachjs.php#recommendationcontainer for recommended pieces.

[28] The second President of the United States (1797-1801), John Adams was an outspoken politician and intense critic of British taxation of the American colonies. John Adams was a self-described "church-going animal" attending the Congregational Church. For additional information and a biography, see https://www.whitehouse.gov/about-the-white-house/presidents/john-adams/. John Adams' writings on religion can be found at www.loc.gov/exhibits/religion/rel06.html#obj157.

[29] Though raised in a conservative Roman Catholic home in France, John (Jean) Calvin converted to Protestantism in 1533 and became a leader of the Christian Protestant Reform movement. His sermons and books, particularly *Institutes of the Christian Religions*, became foundational theological writings for modern Protestantism. For more information, a biography, and recommended books, go to https://calvin.edu/about/history/john-calvin.html.

[30] John Newton was an Anglican minister who vigorously argued against slavery in England during the late 1700s. Newton wrote the poem that became one of the most beloved Christian hymns, "Amazing Grace," in 1772. For a short biography, see https://www.loc.gov/item/ihas.200149085/; for the poem and musical recording of "Amazing Grace," see https://www.hymnal.net/en/hymn/h/313.

[31] Early in his career, Julius Caesar was elected Pontifex Maximus, high priest of the Roman polytheistic state religion. A politician and popular military hero in the first century BC, Caesar fought a civil war to gain control of Rome. Caesar centralized Roman political power and began extensive reforms across the empire. William Shakespeare gave Caesar his famous alleged last words, "Et tu, Brute?" (www.shakespeare.org). For a biography, maps, and video, go to https://www.historyhit.com/a-summary-of-julius-caesars-life-and-achievements/.

- Justinian the Great[32]
- King Henry VIII[33]
- King Ferdinand II and Queen Isabella I of Spain[34]
- Lao-tzu[35]
- Martin Luther[36]
- Malcolm X[37]
- Michelangelo[38]

Memorial statues of King Ferdinand and Queen Isabella meeting with Columbus.

[32] Justinian the Great ruled over the Byzantine Empire (Greco-Roman) from 537 to 565 AD. Under his reign, the city of Constantinople was rebuilt, including multiple Orthodox churches such as the cathedral of Hagia Sophia. Justinian also consolidated the power of the emperor away from the senate, altered church policy, clashed with the Pope on several issues, reformed taxation and civil law, and enlarged his empire to include most land bordering the Mediterranean Sea. For a biography and photos of Byzantine art under Justinian rule, go to https://www.metmuseum.org/toah/hd/just/hd_just.htm.

[33] Raised a devout Roman Catholic, King Henry VIII of England was given the title "Defender of the Faith" by Pope Leo X in 1521. However, by 1534 under Pope Clement VII, when Henry's wife Catherine of Aragon produced no male heir to the crown, the Pope would not grant Henry a divorce. Henry broke away from Catholicism, and the English Parliament passed the Act of Supremacy under Henry's direction, declaring the king as the only authority over the Church of England (Anglican). Henry divorced Catherine and eventually remarried five times, executing wives Anne Boleyn after she produced no male heir to his throne and Catherine Howard on charges of adultery and treason. For further details of Henry VIII's life, go to https://www.royal.uk/henry-viii.

[34] The marriage of King Ferdinand II (of Aragon) and Queen Isabella I (of Castile) unified Spain in 1469. Their armies fought Moorish forces in Andalucia, removing the last from Granada in 1492. Ferdinand and Isabella imposed Catholic religious uniformity via the Spanish Inquisition and expelled Jews and Muslims from Spain. They also financed Christopher Columbus' voyages in efforts to increase trade and territory. For additional information and biographies of both monarchs, go to http://countrystudies.us/spain/7.htm.

[35] Lao-tzu (also Laozi and Lao-Tze) was a sixth-century BC Chinese philosopher who is believed to have authored the religious scriptures known as *Tao Te Ching* and founded Daoism (or Taoism). He is viewed as a deity in Daoism. Confucianists respect Lao-Tzu as a great philosopher and attempt to follow his teachings, such as practicing meditation and chanting scriptures. For a more detailed biography and religious teachings, see https://www.theschooloflife.com/thebookoflife/the-great-eastern-philosophers-lao-tzu/.

[36] Martin Luther, an Augustinian friar within the Roman Catholic Church, dissented in 1517 over Pope Leo X's sale of indulgences and other complaints of corruption and abuses. His 95 Theses pamphlet, said in now-doubted historical accounts to have been nailed to the Catholic church door in Wittenberg Castle, outlined his objections. Pope Leo X excommunicated him in 1521 after he published more pamphlets voicing his objections. In 1537, Luther published a complete translation of the Bible in common German, arguing that every person should be allowed to read the Bible for themselves. His writings inspired the Protestant Reform Movement. For a biography, refer to http://www.bbc.co.uk/history/historic_figures/luther_martin.shtml. For Luther's 95 Theses and other writings, read *Martin Luther's 95 Theses: With the Pertinent Documents from the History of the Reformation*.

[37] While in prison for burglary in the late 1940s, Malcolm X (born as Malcolm Little) converted from Christianity to Islam and joined the Nation of Islam (NOI), which promoted a Black Islamic nation separate from the US. His charisma and strong convictions made him a popular NOI spokesman and minister. In 1964, Malcolm left the NOI to start his own organization (Muslim Mosque, Inc), which preached Islam to all races. After several attempts on his life, Malcolm X was assassinated by three members of the NOI in 1965. For quotes, photos, eulogy, and a biography, go to https://www.malcolmx.com/biography/ or view the film *Malcolm X* (1992).

[38] Considered one of the leaders of the Italian Renaissance, Michelangelo, born in 1475, was a sculptor and painter. His most recognizable works are the statue of David and the frescoes of the Sistine Chapel ceiling, particularly The Creation of Adam. Michelangelo was a devout Roman Catholic but added Spiritualism to his belief system later in life. For photographs of his masterpieces and a biography, go to https://www.michelangelo.org/.

- Muhammad[39]
- Napoleon Bonaparte[40]
- Nicolaus Copernicus[41]
- Oliver Cromwell[42]
- Oskar Schindler[43]
- Pharaoh Akhenaten[44]
- Plato[45]

Representation of Akhenaten.

_____

[39] Muhammad is the last prophet of Islam, and his revelations (beginning around 613 AD) are recorded in the Qur'an. Islam teaches that God (Allah in Arabic) is the only true god, Muhammad is God's prophet, and that prayer, charity, fasting, and a pilgrimage to Mecca are necessary. Within a century after his death, Islam had spread from Muhammad's home in Makkah (Mecca), Saudi Arabia, west to Spain and east to China. For more information about Muhammad and Islam, go to https://www.islam-guide.com/ and https://www.whyislam.org/category/islamicteachings/.

[40] French general Napoleon Bonaparte began his political-military climb in the power vacuum that existed at the end of the French Revolution in 1789. Becoming "first consul" and finally emperor of France as Napoleon I in 1804, he expanded his territory east to Russia and south to Spain. Napoleon was an authoritarian who amassed and used power, but also reformed his empire's laws, in part allowing for religious freedom and equal rights to Jews and Protestants, though he was officially Roman Catholic. In 1815, the English army defeated him at Waterloo. He was captured and exiled to the small remote South Atlantic island of St. Helena (more than 1600 miles or 2600 kilometers west of Angola, Africa), where he died in 1821. For more information on Napoleon, his military campaigns, and his religious beliefs, see https://www.napoleon-series.org/.

[41] Questioning the religious, scientific and political belief of the time that the earth was the center of the universe, Nicolaus Copernicus wrote On the Revolutions of the Heavenly Spheres in 1532. Though Copernicus was a loyal canon (priest) of the Catholic Church, the Church banned his book in 1616. For a biography and detailed discussion of his theories and discoveries, go to https://www.space.com/15684-nicolaus-copernicus.html.

[42] Oliver Cromwell was a relatively unknown, deeply religious Puritan and landowner prior to the English Civil War in 1642. As a member of the House of Lords and an outspoken supporter of the constitutional monarchy that gave little power to the king, Cromwell quickly rose in the Parliamentary Army. In 1649, he signed King Charles I's death warrant for claiming absolute power as his divine right. After Charles' execution, Cromwell won battles against Irish and Scottish armies, leading to the Commonwealth of England, Scotland, and Ireland. Cromwell was appointed Lord General (commander-in-chief) of the Parliamentary army in 1650. In 1653, he declined the crown and was instead made Lord Protector of England (unofficial king). For more information about Cromwell and the English Civil War, go to https://www.historic-uk.com/HistoryUK/HistoryofEngland/Oliver-Cromwell/.

[43] Oskar Schindler is credited with having saved 1,200 Jews from certain death during the Holocaust of World War II. Schindler was a German Catholic industrialist who used his Polish enameling and munitions factories as a way to protect his Jewish workers from being sent to concentration/death camps. His story has been told in the book _Schindler's Ark_ (1983) and the movie: _Schindler's List_ (1993). For quotes, photographs, and a biography, go to https://www.jewish-virtuallibrary.org/oskar-schindler.

[44] Pharaoh Akhenaten reigned in Egypt around 1350 BC, a period of significant social, political, and religious change. Akhenaten disrupted society by moving the Egyptian capital from Thebes to present-day Armana, altering artistic and architectural style, and removing all traditional gods, persecuting believers in the traditional gods, and replacing traditional gods with one god: Aten, the sun god. Much is unknown about Akhenaten, including his cause of death and his burial location, but more biographical details, including discussion of his family, can be found at https://www.arce.org/resource/akhenaten-mysteries-religious-revolution and https://www.nationalgeographic.com/magazine/2017/05/akhenaten-revolutionary-egypt-king/.

[45] Plato was both a mathematician and philosopher in ancient Greece (427-347 BC). He wrote extensively on a wide variety of subjects, including justice, love, virtues, and the immortality of the human soul. For a biography and translations of Plato's writings, go to http://www.philosophypages.com/ph/plat.htm.

- Saladin[46]
- Sitting Bull[47]
- Socrates[48]
- Suleiman the Magnificent[49]
- Walter Rauschenbusch[50]
- William Wilberforce[51]

Sitting Bull.

---

[46] The Sultan of Egypt and Syria, Saladin (1137-1193 CE) was a wise politician and successful military leader. He shocked the western world when he captured Jerusalem in 1187. Though of Kurdish descent and questionably Muslim, Saladin resolutely defended Islam from Christian crusaders. Yet Saladin spared the lives of many Christian captured soldiers, including the French-born King of Jerusalem, Guy of Lusignan. For a timeline, maps, photos, and biography, go to https://www.ancient.eu/Saladin/.

[47] Sitting Bull was both a holy man and the head military leader for the Lakota Nation in present-day South Dakota in 1868. Sitting Bull had visions of his winning battles, but also his losses. General George Custer famously attacked Sitting Bull's encampment on the Little Bighorn River (Montana) in 1876, even though the land was Indian territory under the Fort Laramie Treaty. Custer and his troops were slaughtered. However, gold had been found in the Black Hills, so the US Calvary continued to attack the area's Native Americans, forcing many chiefs to surrender, including Sitting Bull. For a biography of Sitting Bull and additional information on the Lakota culture, go to http://aktalakota. stjo.org/site/PageServer?pagename=alm_culture_chief_bios.

[48] Socrates, an ancient Greek philosopher known for asking questions to teach, was intently interested in the idea of moral character. He often led discussions with students questioning material success and the cultural norms defining "happiness." Socrates is said to have been driven by an "inner divine voice," though not officially rejecting Athenian gods. In 399 BCE, Socrates was convicted and sentenced to death for corrupting the youth of Athens and interfering with the religion of the city. See http://www.philosophypages.com/ph/socr.htm.

[49] A Sultan of the Ottoman (Turkish) Empire, Suleiman the Magnificent (Suleyman I) was born in 1495 and brought prosperity and grandeur to his kingdom. His armies conquered Hungary, Vienna, Iraq, and the Mediterranean port cities of North Africa. Suleiman (sometimes called "The Lawmaker") was highly educated, so when he succeeded his father as Sultan, he enacted standardized written Islamic law. Suleiman was a patron of the arts and architecture, and he is credited with writing beautiful Islamic poetry. For a biography and period art, go to http://www.theottomans.org/english/family/suleyman1.asp and https://www.metmuseum.org/toah/hd/suly/hd_suly.htm.

[50] A minister of the Second German Baptist Church in New York City at the end of the nineteenth century, Walter Rauschenbusch worked to improve life for the impoverished immigrant residents of the Hell's Kitchen community. He preached against poverty, corruption, and crime, which he saw as social sins, and he advocated for social restructuring to end the wealth gap, launching the Social Gospel movement. Rauschenbusch's writings on Christianity and social justice were well-read across America, including *Christianity and the Social Crisis* (1907), *Christianizing the Social Order*, and *The Social Principles of Jesus*. For a timeline and biography, go to https://www.christianitytoday.com/history/people/activists/walter-rauschenbusch.html.

[51] William Wilberforce was a member of the British Parliament and outspoken abolitionist. As a member of the Clapham Sect (Protestant Evangelical) in 1790, Wilberforce began his efforts towards social justice by pushing for working condition reforms within England's factories. He and colleagues began introducing motions in Parliament to abolish slavery in the British Empire, an effort that continued for nearly two decades. In 1807, his motion to abolish the slave trade finally passed Parliament, though existing slaves were not freed until 1833. Wilberforce also worked to provide all English children with education in reading, hygiene, and religion. He was also deeply involved in the Royal Society for the Prevention of Cruelty to Animals. For a biography, go to http://www.bbc.co.uk/history/historic_figures/wilberforce_william.shtml.

This concludes our list of 50 individuals who made a difference throughout history and were motivated by religious concerns. This is not an ancient historical phenomenon, since there are quite a few modern individuals who likewise work for social change and who are motivated by religious concerns. Religious faith and its principles can clearly be seen as one of the core motivators for several of the twentieth century's most prominent agents of social change, as seen in this list:

- **Jimmy Carter**: Although Carter's presidency has often been criticized, the former President of the United States has been known for his faith in diplomacy, the innate goodness of people, and the need for social justice. Elected president in 1976, he negotiated the SALT II treaty between the US and Russia, hosted the Camp David accords that led to a peace treaty between Egypt and Israel, and established diplomatic relations with China. He previously served as the governor of Georgia. Carter believed that the principles taught by Jesus Christ about equity, the value of humanity, compassionate giving, and service to others needed to be put into action. After leaving the presidency in 1981, Carter taught Sunday school at his evangelical Christian church in Plains, Georgia. As the leader of The Carter Center, and winner of the 2002 Nobel Peace prize, President Carter as of November 2020 is a strong advocate for democracy, inexpensive housing, disease prevention, human rights, and world peace.[52]

- **Mahatma Gandhi**: A gentle yet outspoken free-thinker, Gandhi led India's push (1919-1947) for independence from Great Britain through unprecedented non-violent civil disobedience. Gandhi was a humble, prayerful Hindu and Jain believer who practiced his faith daily through diet, self-discipline, and non-violence. His advocacy merely put his faith into action. Professionally trained as a lawyer, an 1893 experience being thrown off a train at a white South African's request awakened his activism. Gandhi fought the prejudice of skin color and oppression in South Africa and India with boycotts, marches, and peaceful means of raising public awareness. He also worked to calm tension between Hindus and Muslims in India, leading to his assassination in 1948 by a Hindu extremist.[53]

- **Martin Luther King Jr**: The person that comes to most Americans' minds when we think of a charismatic individual who acted as an agent of social change is likely Dr. Martin Luther King Jr. He spoke, marched, wrote books, went to jail, and was assassinated as he worked towards the social change of racial equality in America. His Christian faith drove his dream that "one day this nation will rise up, live out the true meaning of its creed: We hold these truths to be self-evident, that all men were created equal" (King 1963). His Christian faith as well as respect for Gandhi's approach also drove his actions of non-violent civil disobedience. Dr. King wrote in several books and sermons that he felt that his work for social change in America was simply an extension of his religious beliefs as a Christian minister.[54]

---

[52] Jimmy Carter, the 39th President of the United States, was unusually active in social change after leaving office. You can read further about Carter at *The Carter Center's* website: https://www.cartercenter.org/about/experts/jimmy_carter.html.

[53] You can learn more about Mahatma (Mohandas) Gandhi by viewing the biographical movie "*Gandhi*" (1982), or you can read a short biography at https://www.biography.com/people/mahatma-gandhi-9305898 and view videos of his speeches at http://www.history.co.uk/biographies/mahatma-gandhi.

[54] Film footage of Dr. King's "I have a Dream" speech can be viewed by going to https://www.history.com/topics/i-have-a-dream-speech. Text of additional speeches and sermons written by Dr. King can be accessed by visiting *The King Center's* website at http://www.thekingcenter.org.

- **Nelson Mandela**: The first freely elected president of South Africa in 1994, Nelson Mandela had spent 27 years (1962-1990) in jail in South Africa for his leadership against racial inequality and South Africa's apartheid system. In 1993, Nelson Mandela—along with former State President of South Africa F. W. de Klerk—was awarded the Nobel Peace Prize for his role in bringing about the end of apartheid in South Africa. Though President Mandela did not speak often of his Christian faith, he was clearly motivated by concerns relevant to social justice. Mandela once stated, "The Good News was borne by our risen Messiah who chose not one race, who chose not one country, who chose not one language, who chose not one tribe, who chose all of humankind!" in his *Address to the Zionist Christian Church's Easter Conference* (Mandela 1994).[55]

- **Mother Teresa**: A Roman Catholic nun who believed that charity and selflessness were the most important parts of being a Christian, Mother Teresa spent most of her adult life drawing attention to India's poorest people and caring for their physical and spiritual needs. She launched a series of internal Catholic clergy movements to better aid the poor, also receiving the Nobel Peace Prize in 1979. Interestingly, she did much of her work amid something of a crisis of faith, fearing that she'd been separated from God and coming face to face with what she called the "painful night" of her soul. Mother Teresa passed away in 1997, and was declared a saint in 2003. She remains a worldwide symbol of compassion to the poor as her historical legacy.[56]

However, these are all historical characters. Does religious faith and its associated religious principles have an impact on today's society? Is religious faith relevant in the hearts and minds of present-day agents of social change? We will now take a look at several other modern-day individuals who are engaging in social change for religious reasons, or at least reasons related to religious concerns. Keeping in mind the ideas of implicit religion—especially the corollary that religious attitudes and behavior extend well outside of religion (Bailey 2011)—and the common religious principles identified by Elgenaidi (2014) and others, we can see that such principles are alive and well. This is particularly true of respect for human life, the value of others, worth and dignity, freedom of religion and conscience, and thought and expression. These ideas are common to most major world religions, and are also present in modern-day activists.

As in the other lists, we have italicized evidence of these common religious principles as they arise in the work of these modern-day activists. Note also that the ideal of "respect for others" also extends in some modern formulations to animals and the environment, which relates to the religious ideal of

---

[55] For additional information, photographs, videos, and historical documents of Nelson Mandela's life and political activities, you can visit https://www.nelsonmandela.org/content/page/collections.

[56] Also known as Saint Teresa of Calcutta. You can read Mother Teresa's biography, quotes, and prayers at the *Mother Teresa of Calcutta Center's* website at http://www.motherteresa.org/ or see an intriguing biography at https://www.catholic.org/saints/saint.php?saint_id=5611.

stewardship over the earth, including those who believe this means taking care of the environment.[57] Environmental activism has been a secular ideal for several decades, of course, but some religious groups—particularly more liberal religions influenced by both this ideology and biblical translation enigmas—see this principle echoed in various religious precepts as well.

In February 2020, Buzzworthy published an article titled "10 Celebrities who use their Fame as a Platform for Change," which listed celebrities who were actively working to make social change. Though the online magazine Buzzworthy is not a recognized professional journal on social change, it is a clearinghouse of American pop culture and celebrity news. Buzzworthy begins their list of celebrities by first stating, "Not all celebrities are gallivanting around town and spending all of their money on fancy cars and jewelry. Many recognize that with great social power comes great responsibility and act accordingly to influence the world in positive ways." Buzzworthy proceeds to list the following celebrities and their causes:

1. **Chance the Rapper**

   Chicago Public Schools has received financial support, $1 million, and encouragement from Chance the Rapper. He has been critical of the Illinois state government's efforts to fund *public education*, particularly in Chicago (https://www.chicagotribune.com/politics/ct-chance-the-rapper-chicago-schools-plan-met-20170306-story.html).

2. **Shailene Woodley**

   While protesting the Dakota Access Pipeline in North Dakota, actress Shailene Woodley was arrested for criminal trespassing and rioting. In her statement to TIME (Woodley 2016) after her arrest, she said, "People … gathered together because they realize that if we don't begin taking genuine steps to *protect our precious resources*—our soil, our water, our essential elements—we will not have a healthy or thriving planet to *pass on to future generations*. I was in North Dakota, standing side by side with Native Americans. You know, those who were here before us."

   Shailene Woodley.

3. **Ashton Kushner**

   Ashton Kushner and Demi Moore are working to combat child sex trafficking. They established the non-profit organization "Thorn: Digital Defenders of Children" in 2009. Thorn's mission statement includes: "Every new platform and new technology could enable an abuser.

---

[57] Christianity has a complex mixed relationship with the environmental movement. In the account in Genesis 1, after creating the earth and the Garden of Eden, in verses 26-28 God gives Adam and Eve what the King James Version calls "dominion" over the animals and Earth alike in verse 26 and tells them to "subdue" the rest of creation in verse 28. Other translations of these passages differ, however, using words such as "reign over" (New Living Translation), "take charge of" (Common English Bible), and "be responsible for" (The Message Bible) in place of "dominion." Instead of "subdue," some translations indicate "master" (Common English Bible), "govern" (New Living Translation), "take charge" (The Message Bible), and "make ye it subject" (Wycliffe). The collective Christian theological approach towards these verses has shifted over the centuries, with various versions of "conquest" ideologies characteristic of the medieval time period down to the nineteenth century, based on a rather literal and imperialistic reading of "dominion" and "subdue." However, with exploration of the language in the translations, many Christian religious groups moved towards more of a "stewardship and responsibility" interpretive framework in the late nineteenth century down to today. See https://www.biblestudytools.com/genesis/1-26-compare.html# and https://www.biblestudytools.com/genesis/1-28-compare.html for more information.

It can also be our best weapon against them. We are dedicated to *ending child sex trafficking and the sexual exploitation of children. And we won't stop until every child, can just be a kid*" (https://www.thorn.org/).

Lily Allen.

4. Lily Allen

Upon visiting a refugee camp near Calais, France and meeting unaccompanied Syrian migrant children, singer-songwriter Lily Allen was heartbroken. She spoke to the BBC, drawing attention to the children's desperate situation. She said, "I think as human beings we have a *responsibility to help those who are suffering*" (https://www.bbc.com/news/entertainment-arts-37607774).

5. Leonardo DiCaprio

A strong advocate for the environment, the actor initiated the Leonardo DiCaprio Foundation in 1998. Its mission statement says, "The Leonardo DiCaprio Foundation is dedicated to the long-term health and wellbeing of all Earth's inhabitants. Through collaborative partnerships, we support innovative projects that *protect vulnerable wildlife* from extinction, while *restoring balance* to threatened ecosystems and communities. LDF's grantmaking program encompasses six focus areas: *wildlife & landscapes; marine life & oceans; climate change; media, science & technology; environment now California program; and indigenous rights*" (https://www.leonardodicaprio.org/).

6. Jimmy Kimmel

In September 2017, when the dismantling of the Affordable Care Act (Obamacare) was under debate in the US Congress, Jimmy Kimmel shared his terrifying personal story on his late-night television show of his newborn son's heart surgery. Kimmel then gave an impassioned plea for *healthcare* in the United States. He said, "If your baby is going to die and it doesn't have to, it shouldn't matter how much money you make." He gave us what he called "the Jimmy Kimmel test," which was, in a nutshell, *no family should be denied medical care, emergency or otherwise, because they can't afford it*" (Bruner 2017).

7. Taylor Swift

Taylor became the voice of silent victims of sexual harassment and violence in 2017 when she counter-sued radio DJ David Mueller over accusations of groping her during a backstage meet-and-greet photo shoot in 2013. When Swift accused Mueller, he was fired and sued her for defamation; a judge later dismissed his suit, but hers was allowed to proceed. Her blunt courtroom testimony and a photo from the shoot convinced the jury, and she won her symbolic $1 countersuit. In an interview with TIME (Dockterman 2017), Swift said, "I acknowledge the privilege that I benefit from in life, in society and in my ability to shoulder the enormous cost of defending myself in a trial like this. My hope is to *help those whose voices should also be heard*. Therefore, I will be making donations in the near future to multiple organizations that *help sexual assault victims* defend themselves."

A view of the Flint River overlooking the Saginaw Bridge in Flint, Michigan, May 2019. In 2014, the city began experiencing dramatic water-quality issues, leading to a public outcry and protests.

8. Bruno Mars

The Flint, Michigan water crisis began in 2014 when city managers stopped using the Detroit municipal water system and instead began using water from the Flint River. Thousands of people were exposed to lead contamination and Legionnaire's disease because of improper water treatment. Numerous YouTube videos also seemingly depicted Flint water as catastrophically tainted, including some showing it as tar-black and even apparently able to be lit on fire due to containing flammable chemicals. Pop singer Bruno Mars came to the aid of Flint's citizens in 2017 by donating $1 million to The Community Foundation of Greater Flint. Mars said, "Ongoing challenges remain years later for Flint residents, and *it's important that we don't forget our brothers and sisters affected by this disaster. As people, especially as Americans, we need to stand together to make sure something like this never happens in any community ever again*" (https://abcnews.go.com/Entertainment/singer-bruno-mars-donates-million-victims-flint-water/story?id=49185690).

9. Bill Gates

In an interview with CNN (Gupta 2017), Bill Gates pinpointed a cure for Alzheimer's disease as his next big target. According to him in the CNN report, "Today, Alzheimer's disease is the most common form of dementia and the sixth leading cause of death in the United States, where a new case is diagnosed every 66 seconds. More than 5 million Americans live with the disease, at a cost of $259 billion a year. Without any *treatment*, those numbers are projected to explode to 16 million Americans with the disease, at a cost of over $1 trillion a year, by 2050." From a *humanitarian* standpoint, Gates has invested $50 million in research. "Any type of treatment would be a huge advance from where we are today." He added, "The long-term goal has got to be *cure*."

10. **Stephen Colbert**

    In 2017, Hurricanes Irma and Maria hit Puerto Rico, which had already sustained some damage from Harvey. Maria in particular caused severe flooding and high winds, producing significantly damaged schools, homes, hospitals, and infrastructure. Launching a *philanthropic effort* to raise money for recovery, Stephen Colbert challenged other celebrities to post awkward photos of themselves on Twitter or Instagram using #PuberMe. For each photo posted, Colbert *pledged* $1000 from his AmeriCone Dream Fund, raising $1 million (https://fortune.com/2017/10/06/stephen-colbert-puberme-hurricane-maria-puerto-rico/).

Of course, it is far from only celebrities who engage in social change. Many talented and motivated yet ordinary and non-famous people also become involved. Since 2007, CNN has published a yearly list of ordinary people involved in social change, calling these people "CNN Heroes." CNN's top ten December 2019 list included:

1. **Staci Alonso**

    In 2007, Staci opened an animal shelter, Noah's Animal House, to *care* for pets of women living at a domestic violence shelter in Las Vegas. Noah's Animal House's mission statement says, "Noah's is a full-service pet facility located right on the grounds of a domestic violence shelter. We look to remove the 'No Pets Allowed' barrier at women's shelters for the courageous survivors looking to *get back on their feet* with their pet by their side" (https://noahsanimalhouse.org/).

2. **Najah Bazzy**

    Najah founded a non-profit organization, Zaman International, to *provide education, job training, food, furniture, and clothing for women and children* in Detroit, Michigan. Zaman International's mission statement declares, "Hope for Humanity. Zaman is committed to facilitating change and advancing the lives of marginalized women and children, by enabling them to *meet essential needs common to all humankind*" (https://www.zamaninternational.org/).

3. **Woody Faircloth**

    Woody created a non-profit organization, RV4CampfireFamily, in 2018 after seeing the devastation of Paradise, California's Camp Fire. He connects displaced families with mobile home owners who are willing to donate their RVs to house homeless families. RV4CampfireFamily's mission statement declares, "14,000 homes were destroyed in the largest wildfire in CA history that left 50,000 residents homeless. RV4CampfireFamily *provides housing to displaced* Paradise families who lost their homes in the Campfire by connecting RV donors and eligible families" (https://rv4campfirefamily.org/).

4. **Freweini Mebrahtu**

    Freweini designed and patented a reusable sanitary pad in 2005 so that girls in Ethiopia would not be forced to drop out of school once they started their menstrual cycles. She works with a non-profit organization, Dignity Period, to *educate* boys and girls about menstruation to remove the cultural taboo and encourage girls to stay in school. Dignity Period's mission statement affirms, "Inequality is a global issue. The school dropout rate for girls in Ethiopia is 51%, while only 30% for boys. When our founders came to understand that menstruation is often the cause of the gender discrepancy in the dropout rate, Dignity Period was born. Our mission is to keep Ethiopian girls in school by ensuring that they have *access* to quality menstrual hygiene products and education" (https://www.dignityperiod.org/).

Dozens of donkey rescue sanctuaries exist across the world, this one on the small Caribbean island of St. Bonaire.

5. Mark Meyers

In 2008, Mark and his wife opened their San Angelo, Texas non-profit donkey sanctuary, Peaceful Valley Donkey Rescue. At about 172 acres, their ranch is the largest donkey rescue facility in the United States. Peaceful Valley Donkey Rescue's mission statement tells us, "Peaceful Valley's Mission is to *provide a safe and loving environment* to all donkeys that have been abused, neglected or abandoned and wild burros under threat of destruction. Peaceful Valley strives to provide solutions to the many problems that plague these wonderful creatures by providing *ethical stewardship* over the funds that are necessary to fulfill this goal. Peaceful Valley, with its nationwide network of ranch facilities and satellite adoption centers, is the country's leader in *rescue, sanctuary, adoption and education*. Together, we can improve the plight of the American Donkey" (https://donkeyrescue.org/our-rescue/).

6. Richard Miles

Richard started his Dallas, Texas non-profit, Miles of Freedom, to assist formerly incarcerated men and women in making a smooth transition back to their families by helping with housing, computers, career training, job placement, identification, and financial literacy. Miles of Freedom's mission statement announces, "Our mission: To *equip, empower, and employ* individuals returning home from prison and *provide support and assistance* for families and communities impacted by Incarceration" (http://milesoffreedom.org/).

7. Roger Montoya

Roger founded his non-profit, Moving Arts Española, in 2008 to provide art classes, free meals, and tutoring to children in a region ravaged by the opioid crisis. The Moving Arts Española mission statement declares, "Build community and cultivate leaders through arts and culture: Moving Arts Española offers visual and performing arts *education*, free *healthy meals*, and *academic support* for the children and youth of Northern New Mexico" (https://www.movingartsespanola.org/).

8. Mary Robinson

In 2011, Mary created Imagine, A Center for Coping with Loss. This non-profit organization uses craft and art projects to *assist children who are grieving* the death of a parent, brother, or sister. The Imagine, A Center for Coping with Loss mission statement announces, "Imagine provides free, year-round *grief support* for children, families, and communities. At Imagine we believe that no child should have to grieve alone. You will find a *community of caring people* who together create a safe, hospitable, clinically sound environment for *mutual support, healing and growth*. Imagine offers peer grief support services to youth age 3-18 and young adults 18-30. Concurrent support groups are provided for parents, guardians, and other adults" (https://www.imaginenj.org/).

9. Afroz Shah

Afroz started a volunteer movement in 2015, then developed a non-profit organization, Afroz Shah Foundation, to *clean up* garbage from the banks of India's ocean shores and rivers. Afroz Shah Foundation's mission statement says, "To Tackle the problem of marine litter, Afroz Shah works every week by doing the following actions on the ground: 1. *Cleanup* of the existing waste like plastic, etc., 2. Stopping the creation of new waste (constant littering), 3. *Empowering* the local citizens to own up to their own waste so that a *long term sustainable solution* is set in motion in the command area where the training is imparted to the citizens, and 4. Involving plastic producers to become a part of the solution to tackle marine litter, involving policy makers, ministers, governance setup and legislatures to develop laws, policy, regulation, rules, guidelines" (http://www.afrozshahfoundation.com/).

10. Zach Wigal

In 2007, Zach founded Gamers Outreach, a non-profit organization that brings video gaming to chronically ill children in their hospital rooms. He also designed a cart for hospital room use that easily brings the gaming console and games to the patient's bed. Gamers Outreach's mission statement tells us, "Let's help others level up! Join our quest to provide kids in hospitals with access to play through the power of video games! Our focus is to *support* kids and teens throughout the healing process as they undergo treatment in hospitals. We equip nurses and child life specialists with the means to make activities and technology accessible. Ultimately, our goal is to create sustainable experiences that produce joy and *minimize trauma* for patients" (https://gamersoutreach.org/).

Though it is difficult to know the exact motivation of the individuals who made Buzzworthy's and CNN's lists, it appears that the specific issues of social change selected by these change agents point to several principles of religious faith. In terms of the common principles cited by Maha Elgenaidi

(2014), we frequently see respect for life as well as respect for dignity, and often respect for others as well. As mentioned earlier, respect for others isn't necessarily other humans, but also animals and ecosystems—even the earth itself, in line with many religious groups' views of the biblical injunction in Genesis 1.

Moreover, as the idea of implicit religion suggests (Bailey 2011), such principles don't even need to tie back to a set of beliefs that are specifically religious in origin. Secular ideology and politics are two other sources that can generate ideas and behavior that resemble religion, thereby accounting for the presence of at least several people on these lists who are not known as specifically religious—and who might even be amused or irritated at the suggestion that their motivations are linked to religion. Individuals don't need to be actual churchgoers to be motivated by principles that are also taught in world religions. Still, religion can definitely be a source of these principles, as it is for many people worldwide.

Yet as with Weber (Berger 1963), some individuals are religiously socialized and practice their beliefs in a priestly and preserving way, while others are more prophetic and innovative. Given Buzzworthy's and CNN's published lists, it seems to be a reasonable conclusion that the principles of religious faith are motivators of social change for at least some present-day individuals. But how do we know that religious faith, and not simply the associated religious principles, is truly at work driving social change in modern society? Let's look at two specific examples (case studies) in Chapters 8 and 9 of two talented and motivated yet ordinary people who are working for social change in today's world.

CHAPTER 8

CASE STUDY: KIM AND CORRECTIONAL LADIES IMPROVING PETS (CLIP)

We live in a country that is addicted to incarceration as a tool for social control. As it stands now, justice systems are extremely expensive, do not rehabilitate but in fact make the people that experience them worse, and have no evidence-based correlatives to reducing crime. Yet, with that track record, they continue to thrive, prosper and are seen as an appropriate response to children in trouble with the law. Only an addict would see that as an okay result.

—*James Bell[1]*

We have covered a great deal of ground so far. We have defined religious faith and considered how it plays a role in social change for organizations, groups of people, and individuals. We have, in particular, reviewed a large number of individuals who have engaged in social change, past and present. However, we haven't yet been able to interview any individual who has tried to make a difference in the world. In the next two chapters, we will do that, starting with Cynthia's friend Kim in this chapter. As we meet Kim, we will see how these ideas apply to individual agents of social change.

To begin, remember our definition of social change in Chapter 1:

> *Social change is a significant alteration of culture, demography, economic pursuits, governmental/political activity, science/technology, and/or social institutions within a society over time.*

And our definition of agents of social change in Chapter 5:

> *Agents of social change are those organizations, groups of individuals, and individuals that take action specifically to cause social change.*

---

[1] James Bell is a lawyer and activist for prison reform and youth justice for African Americans, according to http://www.doonething.org/heroes/pages-b/bell-bio.htm. He is the founder and executive director of the W. Haywood Burns Institute (https://www.burnsinstitute.org/), which works towards improving opportunities and quality of life for young Black males in America, reducing the disproportionate incarcerated population of that group. Source of quote: http://www.betterworld.net/quotes/prison-quotes.htm.

Reading through the list of historical and modern agents of change listed in Chapter 7, it would be easy to assume that social change is something spectacularly huge and immediately impactful across society. It would also be easy to assume that individual change agents need to be charismatic leaders with wide influence and a great amount of financial backing. It might also be easy to assume based on a portion of our discussion in Chapter 5 that individual agents of social change are members of radical religious cults. But of course, these assumptions are not necessarily true, as our case study here will show.

What would society be like if we did not need prisons or chose to not imprison people? For that to happen, there would need to be a great deal of social change.

So, what is necessary? What is necessary to become a "who" of social change? As discussed in Chapter 2, to be an agent of social change, whether an organization, a group of individuals, or an individual (as in Chapters 5-7), you need a motivator. Something must cause you to take action. You may have a complaint or gripe that gives you a sense of discontentment or discomfort, but you need more than a complaint to become an agent of social change.

The motivator must be strong enough to cause you to "get off of the couch" and become a visible, sustainable (often, long-term) agent of social change. In other words, for you to become an agent of change, the area of social change has to disturb your sense of contentment. It has to hit at your passions, at your deeply held beliefs, at your sense of right and wrong, at your identity, or even at your ability to survive.

You also have to be able to envision what society might look like if the social change you desire was to really happen. Of course, your vision might not be correct in real world application or in the long run, but you must have a vision.

Once you have a motivator and a vision, you must take action if you are to become an agent of social change. The action you take does not necessarily need to include marching in a protest or donating a million dollars to a cause. No—your action can be as simple as posting an event's information on your social media page or volunteering an hour or two of your time to a local service organization. Maybe you want to help organize a fundraising event or an outreach/educational event. Maybe you would like to perform some research for a charitable organization or go further with your research as part of an advanced academic degree. Maybe you would like to take a job with a non-profit organization or build a career in a governmental agency. Maybe you'd like to start your own non-governmental organization. And maybe you want to go to Africa to help with the AIDS crisis. It's up to you!

Just remember that your passion, your belief system, your sense of right and wrong, your identity, and your need to survive will point you to your motivator and your vision. And then, it's just a matter of deciding how you want to get involved.

Let's take a look at Cynthia's friend, Kim, and her passion, her motivator, and her action.

Face-to-face Interview between Cynthia (your author) and Kim

June 15, 2020

When first meeting Kim, you would not immediately suspect that she is a powerhouse for social change. She is a small-framed, middle-aged woman with attractive, sparkling eyes and a pleasantly soft voice. Kim appears to be neither strong nor forceful nor intimidating, but instead, she appears to be gentle, kind, and patient. So when I realized that Kim has been the subject of several local newspaper articles[2] and identified as a "legendary local" in a 2014 book,[3] I couldn't stop wondering what about Kim makes her a modern agent of social change. I had to ask and she was kind enough to answer...

Cynthia: Kim, please tell me about your background. What makes you who you are?

Kim: I had a rather difficult childhood with lots of dishonest, unkind men coming in and out of our household. But from these men, I learned what not to be as a human being, and who I really wanted to be. I wanted to be honest and kind, in fact, that is still my goal and it's what I try to model for the people around me: my children, my grandchildren, and my ladies.

Cynthia: Tell me about your ladies and the area of social change that you are involved in. How did you get involved with this specific area of social change?

Kim: I have spent most of my adult life working as a dog trainer and master groomer for elite level dog shows. I loved it, but it was a lot of strain on my body. It's very physically intensive lifting large dogs (salukis) and standing on my feet all day, so I retired early. That's when life got interesting! In 2002, a local veterinarian friend of mine approached me about teaching dog grooming skills to the female inmates at our state prison.

Somehow it just made sense to me to pass on my skills to those who so desperately needed a skill. In college, I had studied law enforcement, so it was like everything in my life was suddenly connected into this new idea!

Cynthia: And how did it work?

Kim: It has been lots of work, good work, but hard work. So much work, that I have retired twice now!

---

[2] Additional information about Kim and CLIP can be found in several Herald & Review newspaper articles: "Clip Program gives Prison Inmates Shelter Pets Chance at Fresh Start," "Decatur Prison's Grooming Program Pampers Pets, Helps Rebuild Lives," "Decatur Prison Looking for Person to run Dog Grooming Program," "Grooming Groomers: Here's how Decatur Prison's Grooming Program Pampers Pets, Helps Rebuild Lives," and "Pet Class is Grooming Success in Decatur's Women's Prison."

[3] Huey Freeman's 2014 book titled "Legendary Locals of Decatur" includes a discussion of Kim and her prison dog grooming salon.

(Continued)

First, I established a dog grooming salon, Correctional Ladies Improving Pets (CLIP), at the Decatur Correctional Center[4] in Decatur, Illinois. And then, I partnered with local animal shelters. Every day, I run my van all over town picking up animals that need grooming, and then take the animals to the prison salon where the ladies learn to care for the animals. When the animals come through the door it's all smiles, hugs, and kisses for each animal and inmate! That kind of positive interaction is rare for prison inmates and for homeless animals.

I have worked hard to connect animals and inmates… it's a healing thing! And I have also worked hard to connect the ladies with skills of gentle kindness, a marketable trade, grooming tools, and a groomer's certification. These things produce a honest confidence, plus a way for the ladies to provide a living for their children so that they will hopefully not return to prison!

Two photos of the grounds of the Decatur Correctional Center where Kim launched her CLIP program. We were unable to provide photos of the inmates in the program due to legal and ethical restrictions. Photo source: Hawkinson, 2020

Cynthia: That's amazing! You are helping two groups in need at the same time! I love it! But let me be honest, I would be very nervous working with state prison inmates. How do you do it?

Kim: Right! Well, you have to keep in mind that many of the ladies are in prison as a result of a very difficult situation, sometimes not of their own making. And you have to know that with a bit of encouragement and skill, we can all make changes in our lives if we want to!

Mind you, I am very particular about who I allow to participate in the program. I interview each lady and ask them some really tough questions. If I don't feel safe or if I don't feel that there is a genuine desire to work and learn, then I don't accept that inmate. For every opening I have, there is a long list of ladies, typically 200, who would like to join the CLIP program. I work with 6 to 10 ladies at a time.

---

[4] For more information about the Decatur Correctional Center, go to the Illinois Department of Correction's website: https://www2.illinois.gov/idoc/facilities/Pages/decaturcorrectionalcenter.aspx.

(Continued)

Cynthia: Well, I still think you are very brave! Do you have a strong sense of religious faith? What does your faith mean to you?

Kim: Oh yes! I attend the local Catholic Church. It is very important to me and my husband.

Cynthia: How did your faith first motivate you to make a difference and what role does your faith play now?

Kim: I truly believe that religion is at its finest when we help others who are in need. It is who we are called to be as Christians!

I really do believe in making a difference. I want life to be different for homeless animals and for incarcerated ladies. If I can help make that difference, then I've done what I believe I have been asked to do by God.

Cynthia: How will you know your effort to make a difference in the world has succeeded?

Kim: As a result of the CLIP grooming salon, thousands of homeless animals have found homes. That makes me very happy! Plus, as a result of CLIP, dozens of inmates have developed skills, passed their groomer's certification exams, and found jobs once release from prison. It's a win-win situation for everyone, including me!

We have a 99% job placement rate, because our ladies learn about customer service, plus animal CPR, first aid, American Kennel Club[5] breed recognition, dog anatomy, immunization requirements, pet illnesses, animal handling safety, and grooming skills. The ladies pass the National Dog Grooming Association[6] exam and take that license, skills, and a $800 grooming tool kit with them when they leave the prison. I have never had an animal or an inmate come back! So yes, I know that I have made a difference!

Cynthia: Wonderful! Are there any other thoughts you would like to share about why you are doing what you do to make a difference?

Kim: Community! My community is where I live my life, and it's where these animals and ladies live their lives. My religious beliefs encourage me to make a difference in my life, my children's lives, but also the lives of others in my community. If you support your community, your community will support you. The local community here has very much supported us at CLIP donating supplies and equipment, and we are absolutely making a difference in our community!

Cynthia: And how does your thoughts about community connect to your religious faith?

---

[5] For information on dog breeds, clubs, and events, go to the American Kennel Club's website: https://www.akc.org/.
[6] The National Dog Grooming Association (NDGAA) certifies groomers through rigorous testing of grooming knowledge, techniques, and abilities using both written and practical skills examinations. Additional information about certification and other NDGAA programs can be found at their website: https://nationaldoggroomers.com/.

(Continued)

Kim: It goes back to what Jesus Christ tells us in Matthew 25:34-40 (NIV):

34 "*Then the King will say to those on his right, 'Come, you who are blessed by my Father; take your inheritance, the kingdom prepared for you since the creation of the world.* 35 *For I was hungry and you gave me something to eat, I was thirsty and you gave me something to drink, I was a stranger and you invited me in,* 36 *I needed clothes and you clothed me, I was sick and you looked after me, I was in prison and you came to visit me.'*

37 *Then the righteous will answer him, 'Lord, when did we see you hungry and feed you, or thirsty and give you something to drink?* 38 *When did we see you a stranger and invite you in, or needing clothes and clothe you?* 39 *When did we see you sick or in prison and go to visit you?'*

40 *The King will reply, 'Truly I tell you, whatever you did for one of the least of these brothers and sisters of mine, you did for me.'*"

It's simple. I want to help others and I want my community to help others as though we are caring for the King, Christ Jesus! And, of course, I want to help animals, too.

Cynthia: Well, thank you for sharing your thoughts with me today. I can see that you are passionately motivated by your faith to make a change in your little community! Wonderful!

So Kim's passion is caring for animals and her community. Her motivator is her religious faith and her desire to care for others as though she is caring for her God. And the action that Kim has taken is developing a program within the local state women's penitentiary and using her skill as a master dog groomer to teach incarcerated women to groom pets, which gives the ladies a marketable skill in hopes that they will not return to prison. A happy bonus to this program has been the adoption of thousands of homeless pets into the community.

Kim decided to take action and do something really big! But she could have started much smaller by holding free dog washes one Saturday a month and encouraging community members to help her. She could have volunteered to groom pets at a local no-kill shelter and trained other volunteers. Or she could have simply donated doggie toys, bags of pet food, and grooming supplies to the local humane society. It was up to Kim how much she wanted to do, how much time she was willing to give, and how much of herself she wanted to invest. She didn't start out with the intention of becoming a powerhouse of social change, but she became one anyway!

Kim's story is further notable in terms of what we have discussed in previous chapters on the religious motivation for social change. Note that Kim saw a need and took the initiative to make changes, in line with our previous discussion of Weber's role of prophets (Berger 1963). These are innovators who don't just keep doing what's always been done, but rather strive for a change they see as necessary. Why does Kim do what she does? She believes it is part of her duty to God to help care for other people and animals. She doesn't necessarily claim an actual religious experience—she doesn't say that God actually told her to found the CLIP program and teach the inmates—but she does believe that it is her religious duty as a Catholic to love and care for her fellow human beings and animals. We saw something similar with Mother Teresa in Chapter 7, where she loved and cared for humanity around her because of her duty to God, even if she at times doubted her calling and even wondered if God was present. Kim, likewise, acted because after reflecting on the religious values she was taught, she felt it was her duty to help the inmates, though she acted in a spirit of love for these women rather than carrying out her duty haltingly and grudgingly. In short, Kim acted because she cares.

Religious socialization is also evident in Kim's comments. For instance, she quoted, at length, Jesus Christ's New Testament instruction to the disciples to care for humanity—including those in prison—as if they were caring for the Lord Himself: "Truly I tell you, whatever you did for one of the least of these brothers and sisters of mine, you did for me."[7] Kim has obviously taken the religious teachings she has acquired into her heart and lives those teachings in the work that she does. This is not only the essence of socialization, but it is her "why" for what she is doing. As we have pointed out throughout the text, the "why" motivates the "who," and Kim's "what" is caring for her fellow human beings in difficulty. Kim has learned through socialization to follow the scriptural instruction to visit/help those who are in prison, and her work stems from that. This desire to help those in prison is her "why," and it comes from her religious faith.

Moreover, we see evidence in Kim's work of Elgenaidi's discussion of the common religious principles: respect for human life, the value of others, worth and dignity, freedom of religion and conscience, and thought and expression. What stands out the most in Kim's interview is her respect for the value of others as well as their worth and dignity—which she intriguingly learned by negative example. She learned she wanted to be honest and kind by her experience as a child being mistreated by adult men who were anything but honest and kind to her. She rose above those circumstances to a better way of being, and seeks to lift others around her who have been in highly negative situations and circumstances themselves. This is respect for others and their inner worth and dignity. We can see also Kim's respect for the lives of the inmates she has taught, as she teaches them skills that will help them succeed in their future lives beyond prison.

Kim needed an organization to succeed in her efforts. CLIP is small and Kim heads it up, and her small organization is a major part of what she is able to accomplish in helping inmates learn to groom dogs. Kim also found it necessary to work with and gain the favor of a highly complex social organization: the Illinois Department of Corrections. CLIP has to comply with correctional regulations and various other guidelines, but joining forces with the prison system allows her to function within the system while helping inmates work towards leaving it behind. She joyfully notes that her program has been highly successful in helping inmates find a better situation in life and stay away from coming back to prison.

Furthermore, Kim's CLIP program to teach inmates dog-grooming skills also exists in a context of various other prison reform efforts nationwide. Various individuals and groups across the nation have recognized the need to help prison inmates by teaching them life skills. Many inmates are in prison because they lack both skills and purpose, so various programs help grant them a sense of self-worth and give them an opportunity to learn and develop job skills that can keep them from returning to prison upon release.

---

[7] Various translations of this passage from the New International Version can be found at Bible Hub. See https://biblehub.com/matthew/25-40.htm. The Contemporary English Version offers this compelling and illuminating alternative: "The king will answer, 'Whenever you did it for any of my people, no matter how unimportant they seemed, you did it for me.'"

Kim's CLIP program compares favorably to various efforts within the general Second Chance Employment movement[8] that helps former prisoners learn job skills and find gainful work. One of these efforts is "Dave's Killer Bread" (DKB), which helps teach baking and other useful job skills to individuals who have served prison sentences. Like Kim, DKB still hires people the organization sees as low-risk to re-offend, but given the experience of their founder, Dave Dahl, they are happy to help those who have had prison records and who wish to turn their lives around.[9] Various religious groups also have prison-ministry capacities, ranging from simply ministers or other representatives who are assigned to help the incarcerated with various needs, including religious questions or assistance or simply providing correspondence or a listening ear. Other groups offer aid to the incarcerated through other means. For instance, James Bell, quoted at the top of the chapter, also heads up a successful organization based in San Francisco to help reduce the rate of young Black men in prison, including various local community intervention efforts such as drug rehabilitation and job-skills training.

In any case, Kim and CLIP fit well with the Second Chance Employment framework, helping inmates learn valuable skills that will help them after they are released from prison. Overall, it is clear after meeting Kim that she learned a great deal from her past life, including in religious terms. Rather than descending into bitterness, Kim used her past experience and religious knowledge as motivation to help others with negative experiences make something better of their own lives. Her religious "why" clearly motivated her to accomplish social change. Next, we will meet another individual, Liz, whose past and religious understanding likewise motivates her in the social change she believes in and works toward.

---

[8] For additional information on the Second Chance Employment movement, go to Good Hire Blog at: https://www.goodhire.com/blog/fair-chance-hiring-is-a-win-win/.

[9] According to their website, DKB founder Dave Dahl was released from prison in 2005, finding no luck in employment until his brother invited him to join him at the family bakery. For more on Dave's Killer Bread, see http://www.daveskillerbread.com/about-us#about-us-1. For several DKB Second Chance Employment stories, see http://www.daveskillerbread.com/secondchances.

CHAPTER 9

CASE STUDY: LIZ AND THEIR STORY IS OUR STORY (TSOS)

Refugees didn't just escape a place. They had to escape a thousand memories until they'd put enough time and distance between them and their misery to wake to a better day.

—Nadia Hashimi[1]

In Chapter 8, we met Kim, an ordinary person striving to make an extraordinary difference for female inmates. Kim is not a charismatic leader of millions; neither is she loud and brash. Yet, her influence is felt as she strives to make the world a better place by teaching female inmates dog-grooming skills. Likewise, those around Liz may not even realize at first that she is there in the same room. She is a quiet, unassuming woman with dark hair and eyes who sits with her young son on the back row and takes in the scene—until it's time to speak. Then, she makes her voice heard—not because it is loud but because it is clear and direct. Hers is a modest voice but strong and confident—the voice of experience—the voice of one who has been there. Liz is an advocate for refugees, and she speaks with authenticity and authority on this issue, for she has been a refugee herself.

Before meeting Liz and hearing her story, let's review a little bit where we've been. We've talked a great deal in our previous text about the "why" that motivates the "who." As we've seen, religious faith is clearly part of the motivation for individuals to participate in social change, and this is no different for Liz, who is a member of The Church of Jesus Christ of Latter-day Saints. In our discussion with Kim, we defined social change as:

A significant alteration of culture, demography, economic pursuits, governmental/political activity, science/technology, and/or social institutions within a society over time.

---

[1] Nadia Hashimi is an author, pediatrician, and activist living in Washington, DC. She has written extensively about the refugee experience and women's rights. Her parents left Afghanistan in the early 1970s for the US, where she was born, though she gained a great deal of insight about the refugee experience through them and included these themes in her work. The source for this quote is https://www.globalgiving.org/learn/12-shareable-world-refugee-day-quotes/. For more information about her and her publications, please refer to https://www.harpercollinsspeakersbureau.com/speaker/nadia-hashimi/. Ms. Hashimi has no known affiliation with Their Story is Our Story, which we cover in this chapter. But those who work with TSOS can attest that the stories refugees tell are often filled with heart-wrenching memories.

© mustafa olgun/Shutterstock.com

Cramped and chaotic refugee camps grew rapidly during the Syrian civil war in 2018.

We also defined agents of social change (as in Chapter 5) as:

> *Those organizations, groups of individuals, and individuals that take action specifically to cause social change.*

Just as Kim fits these definitions, we shall likewise see they apply to Liz as well.

In our previous chapters, we discussed the value of religious socialization and its contribution to a worldview. As people are taught the values of religion, they internalize those values into their own worldview. They begin to see the world in particular ways and according to a certain set of principles and beliefs that have been taught to them. That way of seeing life and experience may well be common to the individual's peer group to some extent, though each individual also adopts aspects of this worldview in ways that are unique to them. In this way, the "who" comes to understand the "why," and that "why" then motivates the "who" to accomplish social change. Religion seems fairly effective at providing that "why."

As part of that "why," many individuals across religious beliefs will learn common religious principles, as we have mentioned before with Maha Elgenaidi's discussion (2014) of various forms of respect as common-religious principles: **Respect for life, respect for dignity, respect for freedom of religion and conscience, respect for freedom of thought and expression, and respect for others.** These values of respect are internalized in the several contexts of the major world religions, as we also saw with Hans Küng's (2004) list of religious principles, which included fair dealing with other people as well as cherishing and loving others. These are principles common to all major world religions and many of the others included in our list in Chapter 4 as well. Through various religious groups, the values that tie back to respect for others are learned and encouraged to be practiced.

Moreover, as we see in the concept of implicit religion (Bailey 2011), these values of respect (and fair treatment and love) don't necessarily have to derive from a specific religious group but may be even more deeply rooted in other social institutions or even society as a whole. A primary implication of this idea is that religion itself may not necessarily even be needed to socialize these values and principles in the short term, though the long-term ramifications of any statement of this type deserve more deliberation and study before reaching or endorsing any conclusions against religious institutions. Other considerations such as social stability, functional needs that religion helps meet, and so forth may give a particular value to religion as an institution that more than compensates for the fact that to some extent, other institutions also do what religion does.

We will see how these ideas and principles work as Liz tells her story and explains why she does what she does. Like Kim, Liz doesn't go about her social change in spectacular or dramatic fashion, though what Kim and Liz do makes all the difference in the world to the people they help. Putting the common principles into practice of humanity and respect towards others doesn't need to be showy or performative, though it is nonetheless effective in making a difference. We also see that individuals have a particular worldview as well as a vision for social change—not necessarily an overt religious experience, but more of a quiet conviction that they are doing God's work or finding their divinely intended purpose. Still, even the quiet convictions still effectively lead the agents of change to become the Weberian prophets (Berger 1963) who alter and innovate. In that sense, Kim and Liz alike are quiet prophets who are committed to making a difference in today's world.

So, as noted in the previous chapter, seeing and understanding the motivation for social change puts the individual agent in motion. Individuals who are motivated then find other like-minded individuals, who join groups that support the change—or if those groups don't already exist, they form them. The groups may grow into organizations that can better meet the objectives of the individual agents of change. As educator and philosopher Cornel West noted in Chapter 5 (1997), individual agents of social change almost inevitably find it necessary to have organizations to bring about the change they seek. Liz likewise found and joined the organization that helps her bring about the social change she wants to see.

Now that we've covered that ground, let's meet Alden's friend, Liz and hear her story, as well as get to know the organization she works with, Their Story is Our Story.

Case Study: Liz and Their Story is Our Story (TSOS)

Interview over email between Alden (author) and Liz

July 29, 2020

I first met Liz in February of 2020 during a presentation given by Their Story is Our Story on our Polytechnic campus at Arizona State University. Since several leaders of and participants in TSOS are also members of The Church of Jesus Christ of Latter-day Saints (though TSOS otherwise has no affiliation with the church and makes no claim to represent it in any way), we started with a discussion at the church institute building just across from campus and then moved to campus for a second address to interested students and faculty.

(Continued)

Liz stood out as the young mom of the toddler-age son who was interested in all the interesting pictures of people, since the presentation materials involved photographs of refugees along with their stories. He happened to be the only child there that day, and I was further impressed when I learned why she had brought her son, as she mentioned in the interview. I spoke with Liz for a few minutes then and was glad when TSOS representatives later recommended her as someone who would be good to speak with for this project.

Alden: Liz, it's good to see you again and talk to you about this project. Please tell me about your background. What makes you who you are?

Liz: What makes me who I am? Two words: nature and nurture. Born in Yugoslavia, into a multi-cultural and multi-religious and multi-lingual family, I was nurtured by the example of my parents from early on that loving and helping other people was simply something you do. We were not rich people, but my parents shared with and lifted up everyone who needed it. If they had one loaf of bread and a gallon of milk, well, we split it and gave half to a family in need. My parents both operated on the Christ-like love principle and it simply rubbed off.

In addition, by nature, I feel that all of us are born with that divine DNA string of empathy and compassion for our fellow beings. It is in our nature as children of God. But I also know that it greatly matters how that string is nurtured during our childhood and whether it develops and blooms into something stronger that carries us through our lives. I had the blessing of being born into a family with parents who were, as Nephi[2] called it, goodly parents. Their example of love, acceptance, fairness, and charity helped develop mine. This is why I take my toddler son to all of my volunteer opportunities and seek those where he can be engaged and learn from [when he is] little on to love, care for, and embrace all people.

Alden: Tell me about the area of social change that you are involved in. How did you get involved with this specific area of social change and this organization?

Liz: As a young girl, I was always involved in service projects, be it with Roma, or families that were not as well off as my family was, or helping friends who struggled with school.

We fled the war in Yugoslavia when I was almost 15. As a refugee child, who was a good student, and a female, I saw the world in a different light. That experience and struggle to stand tall and strong helped me find my passion in focusing my work on helping those who are most often innocent and yet bear the brunt of the burden of any conflict: children and women. As a refugee myself, I have always kept my eye close to developments in the field of refugee work, as well as assistance to children, minors and women in the conflict zones and transitional societies. I had at this point participated in various relief and humanitarian efforts, and volunteered with different refugee-minded organizations, but I was always careful not to attach myself to only one. I was a visiting professor at BYU when TSOS [Their Story is Our Story] came to present and was connected to one of the founders by a mutual colleague. We sort of found each other—my experience, expertise in the field and in NGO [non-governmental organization] management, and their vision and way they are accomplishing it through refugee stories, just drew us in mutually. So, it was by fate, I guess.

---

[2] Nephi is a prominent prophetic character in the Book of Mormon. This reference is actually found in the very first verse of the book, 1 Nephi 1:1. See https://www.churchofjesuschrist.org/study/scriptures/bofm/1-ne/1?lang=eng.

(Continued)

I currently serve with TSOS as Executive Co-Deputy and Director of Strategy. This allows me to assist in streamlining the work TSOS does to make it more efficient as an NGO, in hopes to reach more people and affect greater impact.

Alden: You have a strong sense of religious faith. What does your faith mean to you?

Liz: Everything. It is the light that shines in dark places, and a beacon of hope that helps me see beyond the veil of mortality and through it find mercy and justice for those who this world seems to hurt the most.

Alden: I'm interested in your word "everything." Can you elaborate?

Liz: As a young refugee who lost mom, home and all that was familiar and was thrown into the unknown world, full of strange and unfriendly people, and as a perfect A student who now couldn't understand the material in the strange new language, the Gospel came to the rescue. We were in Austria for about 5 months at the time we met the missionaries and started taking the discussions.[3] I was struggling to hold on to the things my mother taught me about the love of God and I kept praying to see that love in all of the darkness that was surrounding us. The confirmation that I was loved, and the understanding of the plan of happiness[4] saved me from losing that faith and hope my mother instilled in me. It was a light in dark moments since then and has helped me stay focused on the things that matter, and understand that the eternities are fair... That continues to give me hope whenever I get discouraged seeing another innocent life suffer due to the cruelty of humans.

Alden: Thanks for sharing that! How did your faith first motivate you to make a difference? What role does your faith play now in your ongoing effort?

Liz: Because of my faith and knowledge of the Atonement, I can grieve for many beautiful children who suffer needlessly due to our mortal greed and power hunger, and at the same time rejoice knowing that that suffering is followed by a better outcome for them. It helps me forsake hatred and judgment, and let Heavenly Father mete out justice—it allows me to focus on things that matter.

It also gives me the strength to keep pushing when the pushing gets tough and having the faith in our ability to effect change of attitude, emotion and society. It is a great feeling to know "that those that be for us are more than those who be against us,"[5] especially on days when so much of this world seems so cold-hearted and evil.

---

[3] In The Church of Jesus Christ of Latter-day Saints, "the discussions" refers to several lessons involving basic beliefs that church missionaries teach those who are interested in learning more about or joining the church.

[4] "The Plan of Happiness," sometimes also referred to as "The Plan of Salvation," refers to the Church's core teaching about Jesus Christ and the Gospel ultimately being intended for the well-being and happiness of all people who accept it and are therefore "saved." This also helps explain Liz' subsequent reference to the fairness of eternity, since all wrongs are eventually corrected and made right under this plan. An explanation and links are found at https://www.churchofjesuschrist.org/study/manual/gospel-topics/plan-of-salvation?lang=eng.

[5] A paraphrase of 2 Kings 6:16, in which the prophet Elisha and a servant are in peril as a battle looms. According to the account, when the servant expresses his fear, Elisha shows the servant that an extremely large but unseen army of angels stands with them to fight on their side. See https://biblehub.com/2_kings/6-16.htm.

(Continued)

Alden: Can you also tell me more about what specifically about your faith motivates your action? What got you started in advocating for refugees, and how your faith and beliefs specifically played a role in that?

Liz: I know how it feels to not be wanted, to not have a home. I also know that many innocent suffer and bear the brunt of human existence, and that we have been given the responsibility to protect and love as He would. So, my love for Christ and His love for me and His brothers and sisters, motivates me, in hopes to make this world a bit better for those who really have little control over the fact that they have to flee for their lives.

I feel God gave me the experiences He did to use them as an advocate and a voice for change. For whom much us given, much is expected... I was given much.[6]

Alden: How will you know your effort to make a difference in the world has succeeded?

Liz: That is the question…I think that Heavenly Father asks me to push against the rock and give it my all, and then the outcome is in His hands. I know at the end of the day, if the pushing I did that day was all I could give, and that is how I measure. Some days I feel I have contributed, and some days I feel I could have given more…It is a daily struggle. There is also that helper complex, where the more you do the less you feel you have been successful in your efforts. On days when I get stuck in that loop of you could do more, you must do more, I think of Edward Everett Hale's quote, "I am only one, but still, I am one. I cannot do everything, but I can do something. And because I cannot do everything, I will not refuse to do what I can."[7] It is in that "not giving up" that success is measured. And hopefully along the way, we have been able to change someone's attitude toward refugees by sharing their stories, allowing for human to human connection which will impact change of policies, increase integration successes and contribute to a betterment of life.

Alden: Thanks so much for sharing that perspective. Are there any other thoughts you would like to share about why you are doing what you do to make a difference?

Liz: I do it because it is a commandment that we love our brothers and sisters. I do it because I ache for our brothers and sisters with godly sorrow. I do it because it is not an easy fight, but one with thinnest ranks, and someone needs to do it. So, even if I push all my life and see little difference achieved by my pushing, it is still a worthy cause. This notion of making a dramatic difference is beautiful, but sometimes only the side effect, not the actual reason for doing it. I do it because I care for my fellow beings and because I know the weight of the world in dark places. We all need a helping hand, and ultimately, it is how we learn to become divine.

---

[6] See Luke 12:48 for this principle in the Bible, also echoed in LDS scripture in Doctrine and Covenants 82:3 and other passages. See https://biblehub.com/luke/12-48.htm and https://www.churchofjesuschrist.org/study/scriptures/dc-testament/dc/82?lang=eng.

[7] Edward Everett Hale, in Bartlett's Familiar Quotations, compiled by John Bartlett, 14th ed. Boston: Little, Brown, and Company, 1968 (p 717). The quote has some slight differences with the quote we used to open Chapter 7 due to the source. Interestingly, some members of The Church of Jesus Christ of Latter-day Saints on social media have linked a similar quote to Thomas S. Monson, church president from February 2008 to January 2018. Monson often encouraged others to give meaningful service to others in his discourses and likely knew of Hales' statement, but we could find no instance of Monson ever using or paraphrasing this quote.

Liz is an excellent example of a "who" finding a "why" and following through with it. Her motivation was strengthened by her initial experience as a refugee shaping her worldview. She feels that everyone has the capacity for compassion and caring, though she was able to have nurture further develop that nature. Notice her statement that she knew what it felt like not to be wanted, along with her later comment that she knows "the weight of the world in dark places." She, like Kim, came from a background of highly adverse circumstances. Yet faith—as she remarked, "everything" to her—exists to give hope, in her eyes, so that those dark places can be illuminated by the beacon of that hope. With this hope of faith, she trusts that the pain and injustice that exists in this world can one day be made right—and she is willing to work for that.

This not only shows identification with other people, but a depth of caring that helps her understand and relate. Knowing what the refugee experience was like gave her increased desire to want to help those going through that experience. Having been prepared by her life experience, she soon became a refugee advocate. While she was already involved in advocacy and aid relief for refugees by the time of the TSOS presentation she mentioned at Brigham Young University, her contact with TSOS helped her catch the vision of their work. So, she decided to invest her time in serving with them solely. Liz quickly became a valuable member of TSOS with leadership responsibilities. This, along with the initial and ongoing socialization from her parents—which notably "rubbed off" on her—that she was always supposed to help people, share what she had, and care for those around her, helped motivate her to action. The ethos of helping, sharing, and caring gave her the heart and desire to act and continue acting. She does what she does because of that socialization to care for others and share when we have plenty, as well as the resulting worldview that has become part of her.

Not only is this instance of socialization important, but also notably, she expressed her desire to teach her young son similar attitudes and worldview. Liz places a high priority on raising her young son to be a compassionate, concerned citizen of the world who cares for others in need and is willing to share with

This banner, courtesy of TSOS and reprinted with permission, shows the faces of many men, women, and children who have fled oppressive conditions in their home countries and are seeking a new life. Their Story is Our Story tells their stories to raise awareness of the plight of refugees and accepts donations to help them start a new life in their country of refuge.

them in fortune and misfortune alike. As she was taught, and as she was "given much" (for the better and worse), she wishes to give her son the best teaching and education she can. As he receives socialization comparable to what she had, it is her hope that he likewise will carry on the type of work she does. By striving to make this change and innovate in a world that wishes to maintain much of the status quo, Liz typifies the Weberian prophet who resists the priestly impulse to maintain the structure precisely as it is.

Furthermore, Liz also exemplifies the common religious principles we have discussed in previous chapters from Elgenaidi (2014), which likewise resonate with Küng's discussion of religious commonalities (2004). Note that she was not always a member of her current church. She grew up in a different faith tradition, but still learned valuable principles when she was young that still come into play in her work for refugees today. Her comments embody the principles that Elgenaidi spelled out: Respect for life, respect for dignity, respect for freedom of religion and conscience, respect for freedom of thought and expression, and respect for others. Respect for life and its value, dignity and worth of all people, and the worth and rights of others are particularly evident throughout the comments Liz has made and the work that she does. She openly credits her love for Jesus Christ and for her human brothers and sisters all across the world with getting her started in the work she does. It is clear that religion and religious beliefs have played a key role in her motivation and choice to become involved in refugee aid and make a difference in the world.

This is Liz and that is why she does what she does—out of not only a sense of duty to her fellow "brothers and sisters," but also out of a sense of hope and love that as she works, she might play a small part in lifting up others out of darkness into the light—darkness she has felt, but light she has felt as well. This moves her to make a difference. But as we have also said, it's difficult for an individual alone to make a difference in the world. Organizations also facilitate social change, and Cornel West (1997) noted that individuals actually need them to accomplish the changes they wish to make in the world. Let's learn a little more about TSOS.

Visiting the TSOS website at https://tsosrefugees.org/, we find that the front page is filled with pictures of people and names. In many cases, they are the individual refugees' real names, though due to the life situations in which some have found themselves, they are not in a position to give their real names or even to show their faces. Some fear being recognized if their pictures are taken or if their faces are shown in artwork, so they have been obscured and given pseudonyms. Some refugees tell horror stories of seeing loved ones murdered or raped before their eyes. Others recount harrowing escapes from danger or surviving extended periods of starvation or homelessness.

As Nadia Hashimi noted at the top of our chapter, these refugees not only had to leave a place, but they had to try to escape their memories as well—and that second escape is infinitely more difficult than the first. Reading the stories of refugees helps us understand why they left and what dangers they were willing to face, since remaining where they were was even more dangerous than leaving. Being able to tell their stories also helps the refugees be able to cope with what they still remember, and likely always will. The stories help forge a connection between hearer and teller, so that both become more real and human to each other. It is just such a connection that helped motivate Liz to join TSOS and continue a new chapter in her own story, so that the pain of the past would no longer burden the present.

In short, religious faith has clearly played a key role for Liz in motivating her to engage in social change. Principles she has learned throughout her life, especially in the broader religious sense, have helped shape her worldview. Her faith is her hope that continues to help her navigate through a dark and confusing world towards the light, as a refugee dedicated to helping other refugees. She hopes one day that her young son will understand the same lessons and live his life likewise as a caring, compassionate individual who reaches out to others out of love and concern because that is just what people should do for each other. When people do, they all learn each other's stories and see each other as fellow humans. The principles of religious faith clearly underlie and motivate this impulse that leads others to contribute to social change.

Musa's story, also courtesy of TSOS:

In a US-funded project, Musa helped create a database of Afghan military personnel. He also helped identify terrorist spies, which put his own life in danger. He was attacked twice.

Once an RPG fired directly at his car went through one window and out the other without injury to the passengers. He wasn't as lucky the second time. A terrorist on a passing motorbike attached a magnet bomb to his car. The resulting explosion propelled Musa through the windshield. He barely survived. His bodyguards were killed.

From a camp in Greece, where he and his family were halted as they escaped to Europe, Musa mused:

Image courtesy of Elizabeth Thayer and Their Story is Our Story. Reprinted with permission.

"We were a rich family in Afghanistan. My dad was a civil engineer and was earning enough. My mom and I were working. So economically, there was no problem at all.

Nothing. We are not here for economic reasons. We are not here for vacation. We are not here for having fun. We are here due to security reasons.

"I'm educated. I know five languages. I have skills. We all have skills. We can use them. I don't want economic support from any other country. I just need security. I just need peace. I just need to live.

"In a time I was playing with life; I was enjoying, but now life is playing with me. I don't know what is my destiny. Or how long I will be staying here. We will see what will be our destiny and what they will decide for us."

CHAPTER 10
CONCLUSIONS AND QUESTIONS FOR FURTHER RESEARCH

Religious books tell us that when man becomes pure in heart, the lamb and the tiger will live like friends. So long as in our own selves there is conflict between the tiger and the lamb, is it any wonder there should be a similar conflict in this world-body? We but mirror the world. All the tendencies present in the outer world are to be found in the world of our body. If we could change ourselves, the tendencies in the world would also change. As a man changes his own nature, so does the attitude of the world change towards him. This is the divine mystery supreme. A wonderful thing it is and the source of our happiness. We need not wait to see what others do.

—Mahatma Gandhi[1]

As we conclude this book, we want to not only go back over the ground we covered but add advice for those reading our book who would like to make a difference in the world today. We began by asking how the "why" relates to the "who" of social change. We defined social change in terms of functionalism, conflict, and evolutionary perspectives in Chapter 1, and then considered known motivators of social change in Chapter 2. We linked these ideas to a definition of religious faith in Chapter 3, and in Chapter 4 not only explored the landscape of religious faith but also identified several principles and beliefs that are common to all major world religions, which would be likely to be considered by those who act as agents of social change.

In Chapter 5, we saw how these ideas applied to organizations, and considered them in terms of social groups in Chapter 6. In Chapter 7, we considered how individuals past and present have put these ideas into practice when acting as agents of social change. Then in Chapters 8 and 9, we met

---

[1] Mahatma Gandhi, who we met in Chapter 7, was a lawyer, writer, political thinker, and advocate who led India's push for independence from Great Britain in the early 20th century. A more concise paraphrase of the quote above, "Be the change you want to see in the world," is frequently attributed to Gandhi, though no record exists that he actually ever said or wrote that exact phrase. The above quote—possibly the closest approximation to "be the change," if not the actual origin—is found in *The Collected Works of Mahatma Gandhi*, vol. XII, p. 158. (https://www.gandhiheritageportal.org/cwmg_volume_thumbview/MTI=#page/194/mode/2up). See the relevant Quote Investigator discussion at https://quoteinvestigator.com/2017/10/23/be-change/, which traces the much shorter paraphrase of the quote as it apparently emerged from the work of several 1970s writers and activists.

Changing the world may first require a change in attitude.

Kim and Liz, two ordinary-yet-extraordinary agents of social change. Both Kim and Liz, as the "who," state that they are acting for reasons that clearly include their religious faith—the "why." It seems clear that whether we are looking at functional, conflict, or evolutionary views of social change, religion can clearly serve as a key part of the "why" that motivates the "who."

Of course, we cannot conclude based on the case studies of Kim and Liz alone that religion can and does play a distinct part in social change. This modest piece of research has only scratched the proverbial surface of this complex issue. We hope that by considering how religion has clearly operated in the lives of many other individuals, groups, and organizations, that we have presented a compelling case to examine the possibility that religious faith is a distinct motivator of social change—and in any case, religious faith, beliefs, behavior, and motivation all deserve more consideration in the discourse of social change than currently occurs. Religion makes a distinct difference to a wide variety of individuals across the world, and as we mentioned earlier, somewhat contrary to Marx's assessment about religion being the opium of the people (1844), it motivates some people to make changes rather than simply accept their situation in life.

How does this happen? We have considered religious socialization as part of the answer to this question. People who believe in religion are taught a set of beliefs, attitudes, actions, and worldview (Sherkat 2003), and the possibility of religious believers becoming an agent of social change suggests that some believers have been taught to think and act in particular ways as part of their religious background. Moreover, this religious-socialization component need not start at birth, since neither Kim nor Liz remains in the same faith or life situation they were to start life. In fact, both experienced adverse circumstances early on and reacted to them with their later motivation to change.

Exactly what beliefs and behaviors would need to be socialized to result in social change remains something of an open question, though Kim and Liz certainly imply—and our review of past and present individual agents of change likewise suggests, along the lines of Weber's distinction between tradition-minded priests and innovative prophets (Berger 1963)—that a predisposition to action and putting belief into practice would be crucial in becoming an agent of social change. In fact, both participants cited scripture or alluded to scriptural teachings to explain their position on making a difference in the world. Religion is clearly a core part of their motivation for doing what they do. We can't generalize based on a sample of two, but they do provide a small degree of evidence that socialization to make a difference in the world is a distinct possibility. This intriguing question clearly needs further consideration and study—along with how prevalent this tendency would be and in which religions it would best function—but the question is nonetheless well worth considering.

Even further, we have seen that agents of social change—organizations, groups, and individuals alike—tend to embody a set of common religious principles and respect for others (Elgenaidi 2014). Persistently, the themes Elgenaidi identified tend to emerge when considering activism motivated by religion or religious-type rationales: Respect for life, respect for dignity, respect for freedom of religion and conscience, respect for freedom of thought and expression, and respect for others. Throughout our examination in Chapters 5-9, we have repeatedly seen that the themes of respect for life, dignity, and others—considered broadly as people, animals and other living things, and even the Earth itself—tend to emerge in activism that is related to these broad concerns that are echoed in religious attitudes. The concept of implicit religion (Bailey 2011) further indicates that religious concerns can and do exist well outside of the openly religious context, so we see those forms of respect echoed in the activism of even those who would not necessarily consider themselves religious in any sense.

Our case studies also show a particularly human aspect of the "why" motivating the "who" in terms of religion. Both are relatively quiet people who seem ordinary, yet are making extraordinary efforts to change others' lives for the better. As was the case with both Kim and Liz, social change doesn't have to be spectacular or dramatic to be effective. Social change may be as subtle as offering a smile to others, letting someone else know you care, giving much-needed praise or effective coaching, or telling others your inspiring story. However, the motivation—our "why" of social change—is important for those who act as agents of social change. In fact, we might even call it crucial or necessary. Without the "why" of social change, the "who" sees no reason to act or intervene, and nothing different happens. But when the "who" finds the "why," the worldview shifts.

Even more importantly, the individual sees the vision of what should be—what must be—and there is a reason to act. This is not necessarily an overt religious experience, since individuals may well simply see what needs to change in their own minds. Of course, a few individual agents of social change have credited various sorts of compelling experiences with helping them see what needs to change, as seen with Joan of Arc. Yet a larger number of individual agents of social change may still feel themselves to be doing God's work, as we saw with Dr. Martin Luther King Jr., whether they perceive such an experience in a dramatic or subtle way. The subtle experiences—the feelings of "being called," understanding what presumably must happen, thoughts or feelings of inspiration, simply seeing and understanding their role and accepting their duty, and so forth—are by far the most common. They become the Weberian prophets (Berger 1963), working to change and innovate in the world around them.

As we conclude this study, we want to list a set of questions for further research. These are not only notes for ourselves on issues that we could follow up with in a later edition, but also suggestions for the social-science-inclined who read this book about further research that could be done. If others wish to explore these issues, that helps our collective understanding of these issues. We have previously noted a few questions that are worth further exploration, the first in our notes in Chapter 6 and another just above.

The "who," "what," and "why" of social change is a human story with religious faith commonly visible.

In Chapter 6, readers may recall we briefly raised the question that if implicit religion is real, whether this means that all activism might be inherently religious in that implicit-religion sense (Bailey 2011). Further exploring this issue may raise a whole new set of questions and concerns, but they are still well worth asking and exploring. Second, just above, we wondered about the connection between socialization and activism. How are activists socialized, and what differences exist in religious activism? Can we find common themes in the socialization of activists, and how prevalent is this phenomenon?

We might also suggest that since case studies are hardly able to be generalized, more extensive studies are necessary to find whether Kim's and Liz' experiences, as well as those we cited of our notable religiously motivated individuals, can be generalized to larger populations. In addition, we should find out more about the link between organizations and individuals. How much can individuals accomplish on their own before they need a larger group or organization to help create more social change? How much of the organization reflects the individual, and what tensions arise between individuals and organizations as they work for change?

In addition, in Chapter 6, we also pointed out a possible relationship between religious experience and activism. It seems quite clear that dramatic and spectacular religious experiences such as that claimed by Joan of Arc (Biography.com; BYUtv 2015) are far from the norm. Rather, most individuals who are motivated by directly religious concerns experience much more subtle feelings of religious experience, such as a small, quiet confidence that they are doing what God wants them to do. Dr. Martin Luther King, Jr. (AFSCME 2020) is one of these; our case studies Kim and Liz are two others who feel confident they are doing God's work. Mother Teresa may be a little in the middle on this, as she did claim an initial profound revelatory experience of knowing Jesus wanted her to "Come be my light" to the poor and oppressed of India (Catholic.org 2020). She likewise strove to do God's will as she understood it, though she felt depressed and weighed down and sometimes felt distant from any divine presence, still putting her in the "quiet confidence" category (*Ibid.*). Yet, since religious experience overall is not always claimed even by religiously motivated activists, the link between religious motivation and religious experience still needs further exploration to determine how frequent, constant, or strong it may be.

Finally, also as indicated in Chapter 6, the role of media in social activism is an interesting area of further exploration. Since socialization is an important part of the "why" and the "who," and media are certainly part of socialization, how do media help socialize those who are motivated to engage in social change? Does this socialization differ from religious to non-religious? How do activists learn about other activists and gain insights from them? Media of all kinds can be expected to play some sort of role in developing interest and motivation for social change—after all, even this very book itself is media!—and media involvement, what kinds, how much, and so forth constitute really good questions to explore further.

In sum, referring back to the Gandhi quote at the top of the chapter, everyone is capable of changing the world to some extent. Even if the well-known aphorism, "Be the change you want to see in the world," may not have actually come from Gandhi, the thought resonates with his essential philosophy. We are all part of the same world, and when we change, the world changes. As long as the world is full of tigers trying to eat the lamb, there will be more tigers and fewer lambs. When we connect with our inner nature, become more like the lamb, work against the tigers within ourselves, and teach others to be more like lambs than tigers, the world cannot help but change. All along, the "why" will continue to motivate the "who."

Cynthia: Those were fascinating case studies! Both Kim and Liz really showed how religion helps motivate social change, so our thanks to them for letting us interview them. We've also been on quite a journey. Now it looks like we have reached the end of our book. What concluding thoughts do you have, Alden?

Alden: It's a good thing you asked! First of all, you did such a wonderful job finding and compiling all those resources and websites throughout the book, I guess I couldn't help but add a few of my own. Curiously, things like this often tend to happen when I'm working on projects, but I'm forever finding material I wish I had included after it's too late to include it. This project may well be no exception—though happily, there are a handful of helpful resources I did find, barely before it became too late. For instance, not long before our publication deadline, while madly typing away on my laptop and looking for supplementary material for Chapter 9, I stumbled across a website that we actually could have spotlighted closer to the beginning—an amazing resource for making a difference in today's world: The Emily Fund at http://www.emilyfund.org/.

This resource is named for Emily Silverstein, a brilliant 19-year-old student and activist at Gettysburg College in Pennsylvania who was horrifically killed in April 2009 in an apparent episode of dating violence. The site is set up in her honor and includes a great many wonderful resources. They include http://www.doonething.org, which does something similar to what we've done in our book at one point, giving the backgrounds of various activists and efforts. This is a good clearinghouse for information on social change. It is heart-rending what happened to Emily Silverstein, but the development of these resources is a wonderful tribute to her and gives meaning and legacy to her life.

As a conclusion to our theme about religious faith and social change, I also thought it would be useful to include a note about some religion sites I'm familiar with that encourage ways to serve and make a difference. These include the following resources for those interested:

- International Christian Aid (http://www.icaid.org/), a site sponsored by a non-denominational Christian organization offering humanitarian assistance to third world countries, emphasizing hunger relief for children.

- Just Serve (https://www.justserve.org/), a site sponsored by The Church of Jesus Christ of Latter-day Saints, which serves as a clearinghouse for local community service opportunities for anyone wanting to make an immediate difference.

- Islamic Relief (https://www.islamic-relief.org/), an international organization based in London sponsored by various Muslim affiliates and individuals. The group provides humanitarian assistance to various causes across the world, emphasizing emergency relief, gender justice, and local health and empowerment.

- Sikh Aid (https://unitedsikhs.org/disaster-relief-sikh-aid/), a grass-roots organization that began in New York but has spread to many different countries across the world, providing disaster relief and advocating for human rights as well as education and empowerment.

(Continued)

Cynthia: Amazing! Those look like good resources, and they further underline what we've been saying all along about the relationship of religious faith and social change. Many organizations will engage in relief efforts and helping the world become a better place simply because that's just who they are. As I've said before, I am an advocate because that is simply who I am. I want to encourage all who feel motivated to make the world a better place to simply get started. I hope this book has made a difference!

In light of the 2020 grassroots movement for policing/criminal justice reform and improvement on American racism, I'd like to share an analogy that a wise colleague once told me as a result of my questions about the social justice of power and privilege:

The Pretty Girl Analogy

When a pretty high school girl walks into a room of less pretty girls, she has a choice: 1) She can make fun of the other girls, ignore them, oppress them. She will be the pretty girl but no one will truly like her, though some may choose to befriend her out of fear of becoming her target or in hopes of gaining some of her privilege and power. Or 2) She can lift up the other girls by highlighting their skills and abilities, and empowering them to be the significant individuals that they really are. In this way, she is not only privileged, powerful, and pretty, but also generous and likeable with lots of genuine friends. Either way, she is no less pretty, because she is, in fact, already pretty. Her "prettiness" is not dependent on other girls being less pretty.

© Dean Drobot/Shutterstock.com

Beautiful and happy people are all the more beautiful and happy for lifting each other up.

In the same way, those of us in America with power and privilege, the American white upper-middle class, can choose to oppress those with less power and privilege, but conflict and anger will continue to bubble to the surface. The oppressed will not be happy, but some may sidestep the issue or stay quiet out of fear or in hopes of gaining some of the white privilege and power. Or the American white upper-middle class can choose to empower the less privileged to use their skills and abilities so that they too can be successful. We will be no less important if we raise up others who are oppressed. In fact, we become more than ourselves. We become generous, likeable agents of social change.

(Continued)

Either way, the American white upper-middle class is no less privileged or powerful, because we are already successful. My success is not dependent on someone else's failure. In America, there are enough resources, opportunities, dreams, and market-share for everyone to be successful!

Alden: That's a wonderful analogy. Thanks for sharing that, Cynthia! I think we fall into a trap as people and society far too often: We think everything has to be a zero-sum game. If I win, you lose, and if you win, I lose? No, that's not how it always works, and in fact, socially, that's rarely if ever true. People can and should help each other succeed, and society works better when we do exactly that. Most wins and losses don't come at each other's expense. As John Greenleaf Whittier once wrote, "I'll lift you and you lift me, and we'll both ascend together."[2] That's how a civil society works.

Cynthia: Yes, I agree! Civil society is at its best when people value each other and work together for everyone's benefit. In fact, many agents of change are doing exactly that, valuing people and working towards the benefit of others… working towards the better society that they can envision.

And speaking of working together, I want to thank you for agreeing to work on this project with me! This has been a long and wonderful journey!

Alden: Oh, you're welcome, and thanks for the invitation. No problem at all, Cynthia. This has been a tremendous adventure!

Cynthia: Yes, it has. Best wishes to you and all who have just read this book! Thanks for being part of our journey as well, and whatever else you do, please go out and make a positive difference in the world!

© emerald_media/Shutterstock.com

* The views we express in these conversations are our own as private citizens and are not meant to represent the perspectives or policies of any other person, social group, or institution, including those of the religious organizations we attend or of our employer.

---

[2] John Greenleaf Whittier was an American poet who briefly dabbled in politics and was an ardent Abolitionist. He lived from 1807-92 in New England and many of his poems reflect the quiet beauty of the New England countryside. For more on his life, see https://poets.org/poet/john-greenleaf-whittier. This quote comes from https://www.azquotes.com/quote/313947.

REFERENCES

"1 Nephi 1:1." *The Book of Mormon: Another Testament of Jesus Christ.* Published by The Church of Jesus Christ of Latter-day Saints, Salt Lake City, Utah. Accessed September 28, 2020. https://www.churchofjesuschrist.org/study/scriptures/bofm/1-ne/1?lang=eng.

"10 Celebrities Who Use Their Fame as a Platform for Change." Buzzworthy, February 24, 2020. https://www.buzzworthy.com/10-celebrities-use-fame-for-change/.

"46 Weird Laws Still on the Books." Mental Floss, April 11, 2013. https://www.mentalfloss.com/article/50041/50-weird-laws-still-books.

ABC News. ABC News Network. Accessed August 3, 2020. https://abcnews.go.com/Entertainment/singer-bruno-mars-donates-million-victims-flint-water/story?id=49185690.

"Abolishing Abortion: The History of the Pro-Life Movement in America." Abolishing Abortion: The History of the Pro-Life Movement in America | The American Historian. Accessed July 26, 2020. https://www.oah.org/tah/issues/2016/november/abolishing-abortion-the-history-of-the-pro-life-movement-in-america/.

Adams, John. "Religion and the Founding of the American Republic Religion and the Federal Government, Part 1." Religion and the Federal Government, Part 1 - Religion and the Founding of the American Republic | Exhibitions (Library of Congress), June 4, 1998. http://www.loc.gov/exhibits/religion/rel06.html.

"Adolf Hitler." Biography.com. A&E Networks Television, June 3, 2020. https://www.biography.com/dictator/adolf-hitler.

"Afroz Shah Foundation, Beach Cleanup, Social Work Foundation." Afroz Shah Foundation. Accessed August 3, 2020. http://www.afrozshahfoundation.com/.

Alami, Mona. August 26, 2018. "Druze Communities Face a Regional Decline in Influence." The Fikra Forum: Washington Institute. Accessed September 2, 2020. https://www.washingtoninstitute.org/fikraforum/view/druze-communities-face-a-regional-decline-in-influence.

Al Jazeera. "Bahrain Targets Shia Religious Sites." News | Al Jazeera. Al Jazeera, May 14, 2011. https://www.aljazeera.com/video/middleeast/2011/05/201151311201638934847.html.

"All About Religion." Allaboutreligion.org. Accessed September 1, 2020. https://www.allaboutreligion.org/.

"The American Indian Movement, 1968-1978." The American Indian Movement, 1968-1978 | DPLA. Accessed August 3, 2020. https://dp.la/primary-source-sets/the-american-indian-movement-1968-1978.

American Kennel Club. Accessed August 6, 2020. https://www.akc.org/.

Anolik, Ruth Bienstock and Howard, Douglas L. *The Gothic Other: Racial and Social Constructions in the Literary Imagination.* McFarland & Company, Inc. 2004.

"The Antiwar Movement." Independence Hall Association. Accessed August 2, 2020. https://www.ushistory.org/us/55d.asp.

"The Arab Spring in Egypt." Religious Literacy Project. Accessed July 29, 2020. https://rlp.hds.harvard.edu/faq/arab-spring-egypt.

ARDA (Association of Religion Data Archives). 2020. "Church of Christ, Scientist." Accessed September 2, 2020. http://www.thearda.com/Denoms/D_1126.asp.

Argyle, Michael. 2009. "The Psychological Perspective on Religious Experience." *Religious Experience Research Center*: Westminster College, Oxford, UK.

"Authors: John Greenleaf Whittier." AZ Quotes. Accessed September 2, 2020. https://www.azquotes.com/quote/313947.

Bach, Natasha. "Colbert's Awkward Celebrity Photo #PuberMe Campaign Raises $1 Million for Puerto Rico." Fortune. October 6, 2017. https://fortune.com/2017/10/06/stephen-colbert-puberme-hurricane-maria-puerto-rico/.

Bailey, Edward. 2011. "Implicit Religion." *The Oxford Handbook of the Sociology of Religion*, ed. Peter Clarke. Oxford, UK: University of Oxford Press.

Barrett, William P. "The Largest U.S. Charities For 2016." Forbes. Forbes Magazine, December 16, 2016. https://www.forbes.com/sites/williampbarrett/2016/12/14/the-largest-u-s-charities-for-2016/.

Bartlett, John. 1968. *Bartlett's Familiar Quotations*, 14th ed. Boston: Little, Brown, and Company, 1968.

"Basic Repertoire List - J.S. Bach." Classical Net. Accessed July 31, 2020. http://www.classical.net/music/comp.lst/bachjs.php.

Basirico, Laurence A. *Introduction to Sociology*, 4th Edition. BVT Publishing, 2009.

BBC News, May 28, 2010. "Who are the Ahmadi?" Accessed September 2, 2020. http://news.bbc.co.uk/2/hi/south_asia/8711026.stm.

"Be the Change You Wish to See in the World." Quote Investigator. Accessed September 2, 2020. https://quoteinvestigator.com/2017/10/23/be-change/.

Bellah, Robert. 1967. "Civil Religion in America." Daedalus, vol. 96, no. 1, pp. 1-21. Hyperlink: Bellah, Robert N. "Civil Religion in America." Daedalus 96 (1967): 1–21.

Bellah, Robert N. *Religion in Human Evolution from the Paleolithic to the Axial Age*. Cambridge, MA: Belknap Press of Harvard University Press, 2011.

Berger, Peter. 1963. "Charisma and Religious Innovation: The Social Location of Israelite Prophecy." *American Sociological Review*, vol. 28, no. 6, pp. 940-50.

Berger, Peter. 1979. *The Heretical Imperative: Contemporary Possibilities of Religious Affirmation*. New York: Anchor Books.

Berger, Peter. 1990. *The Sacred Canopy: Elements of a Sociological Theory of Religion*. New York: Anchor Books.

Berkeley Center staff. Undated. "Demographics of Buddhism." Accessed September 2, 2020. https://berkleycenter.georgetown.edu/essays/demographics-of-buddhism.

Berry, Ciara. "Henry VIII (R.1509-1547)." The Royal Family, August 3, 2018. https://www.royal.uk/henry-viii.

Better World Quotes. "Prison Reform Quotes." Accessed September 2, 2020. http://www.better-world.net/quotes/prison-quotes.htm.

Beyer, Catherine. June 25, 2019. "The Beliefs and Practices of Rastafarianism." LearnReligion.com. Accessed September 2, 2020. https://www.learnreligions.com/rastafari-95695.

Biblehub.com. "2 Kings 6:16." Accessed September 2, 2020. https://biblehub.com/2_kings/6-16.htm.

Biblehub.com. "Luke 12:48." Accessed September 2, 2020. https://biblehub.com/luke/12-48.htm.

Biblehub.com. "Matthew 25:40." Accessed September 2, 2020. https://biblehub.com/matthew/25-40.htm.

"Billy Graham Evangelistic Association." Accessed August 2, 2020. https://billygraham.org/.

"Biography. Malcolm X." Accessed July 31, 2020. https://www.malcolmx.com/biography/.

"Black Lives Matter." Accessed June 22, 2020. https://blacklivesmatter.com/about/.

"Blue Laws." *Sunday, Court, Supreme, and Closing - JRank Articles*. Accessed August 13, 2020. https://law.jrank.org/pages/4795/Blue-Laws.html.

"Bob Marley Official Website." Accessed July 30, 2020. https://www.bobmarley.com/.

The Book of Mormon: Another Testament of Jesus Christ. Published by The Church of Jesus Christ of Latter-day Saints, Salt Lake City, Utah. Accessed September 2, 2020. https://www.churchofjesuschrist.org/study/scriptures/bofm?lang=eng.

Boys & Girls Clubs of America - Providing millions of kids and teens a safe place to develop essential skills, make lasting connections and have fun. Accessed August 2, 2020. https://www.bgca.org/.

"A Brief History of Disability Rights and the ADA," June 1, 2020. https://ability360.org/livability/advocacy-livability/history-disability-rights-ada/.

"A Brief Illustrated Guide to Understanding Islam." Islam Guide: A Brief Illustrated Guide to Understanding Islam, Muslims, & the Quran. Accessed August 1, 2020. https://www.islam-guide.com/.

Bromley, David G., and J. Gordon Melton. "Reconceptualizing Types of Religious Organization." *Nova Religio* 15, no. 3 (2012): 4–28. https://doi.org/10.1525/nr.2012.15.3.4.

Bruner, Raisa. "Read the Passionate Jimmy Kimmel Healthcare Monologue." Time. Time, September 20, 2017. https://time.com/4949522/jimmy-kimmel-healthcare-transcript/.

Calvin, Jean. 1845 (orig. 1536). *The Institutes of the Christian Religion*. Trans. Henry Beveridge. Online courtesy of Christian Classics Ethereal Library. Accessed September 28, 2020. https://www.ccel.org/ccel/calvin/institutes.html.

Caminiti, Susan, special to CNBC.com. "The Top 10 Charities Changing the World in 2016." CNBC. CNBC, November 29, 2016. https://www.cnbc.com/2016/11/29/the-top-10-charities-changing-the-world-in-2016.html.

Campbell, Joseph, with Bill Moyers. 1988. *The Power of Myth. New York: MJF Books.*

"Cao Dai." 2020. Encyclopedia.com. Accessed September 2, 2020. https://www.encyclopedia.com/philosophy-and-religion/other-religious-beliefs-and-general-terms/miscellaneous-religion/cao-dai.

"Caring Voice Coalition." Accessed May 20, 2020. https://www.caringvoice.org/.

Carl, John D. *Think Sociology*. Prentice Hill, 2010.

Carnegie Corporation of New York. "*The Gospel of Wealth.*" Accessed September 2, 2020. https://www.carnegie.org/about/our-history/gospelofwealth/.

"Carry Nation Biography (Carrie Nation, Carry A. Nation)." Alcohol Problems & Solutions, October 31, 2019. https://www.alcoholproblemsandsolutions.org/carry-nation-biography-carrie-nation/.

Cartwright, Mark. "Genghis Khan." Ancient History Encyclopedia. Ancient History Encyclopedia, July 28, 2020. https://www.ancient.eu/Genghis_Khan/.

Cartwright, Mark. "Saladin." Ancient History Encyclopedia. Ancient History Encyclopedia, July 29, 2020. https://www.ancient.eu/Saladin/.

Catholic Online. "St. Teresa of Calcutta—Saints and Angels." Last accessed September 1, 2020. https://www.catholic.org/saints/saint.php?saint_id=5611.

Cesar Chavez Foundation. Accessed July 30, 2020. https://chavezfoundation.org/.

"Charity Ratings: America's Most Independent, Assertive Charity Watchdog." CharityWatch. Accessed August 2, 2020. https://www.charitywatch.org/.

"The Chicago School of Media Theory Theorizing Media since 2003." The Chicago School of Media Theory RSS. Accessed August 19, 2020. https://lucian.uchicago.edu/blogs/mediatheory/keywords/dialectic/.

"The Chicano Civil Rights Movement." The Library of Congress. Accessed August 2, 2020. https://www.loc.gov/item/ihas.200197398/.

The Church of Jesus Christ of Latter-day Saints. "Plan of Salvation." Gospel Topics essays. Accessed September 2, 2020. https://www.churchofjesuschrist.org/study/manual/gospel-topics/plan-of-salvation?lang=eng.

The Church of Jesus Christ of Latter-day Saints. "Worldwide Statistics." Newsroom of the Church. Accessed September 2, 2020. https://newsroom.churchofjesuschrist.org/facts-and-statistics.

"Civil Rights Movement." A&E Television Networks, August 21, 2018. https://www.history.com/topics/civil-rights-movement.

"CNN Honors 10 Men and Women for Making the World a Better Place." CNN Cable News Network, December 8, 2019. https://www.cnn.com/2019/10/30/world/cnn-heroes-top-ten-2019/index.html.

Cohen, Bernard. 1963. *The Press and Foreign Policy*. New York: Harcourt.

Cohen, Jonathan. 2011. "Audience Identification with Media Characters." *Psychology of Entertainment*, ed. Jennings Bryant and Peter Vorderer. New York: Routledge.

The Collected Works of Mahatma Gandhi. Gandhi Heritage Portal. Accessed September 2, 2020. https://www.gandhiheritageportal.org/cwmg_volume_thumbview/MTI=#page/194/mode/2up.

"Collections." Nelson Mandela Foundation. Accessed August 3, 2020. https://www.nelsonmandela.org/content/page/collections.

"Commonality Quotes." (Rabbi Lord Jonathan Sacks.) Accessed September 1, 2020. https://www.azquotes.com/quotes/topics/commonality.html.

"Confucius," March 4, 2020. https://www.biography.com/scholar/confucius.

"Constantine the Great: The Emperor Who Created Europe." HistoryExtra. Accessed July 30, 2020. https://www.historyextra.com/period/roman/constantine-great-life-facts-christian-roman-emperor-europe/.

Copernicus, Nicolaus. *On the Revolutions of the Heavenly Spheres*. Amherst: Prometheus Books, 1995.

"Cornel West Quotes." Accessed August 2, 2020. https://www.brainyquote.com/quotes/cornel_west_777699?src=t_social_change.

"The Creation of 'Amazing Grace.'" The Library of Congress. Accessed July 31, 2020. https://www.loc.gov/item/ihas.200149085/.

Cruickshank, Saralyn. "The Rise and Accidental Fall of the Berlin Wall." Hub: Publication of Johns Hopkins University. Accessed September 1, 2020. https://hub.jhu.edu/2019/11/05/berlin-wall-mary-elise-sarotte/.

"Culture." Merriam-Webster.com. Accessed September 28, 2020. https://www.merriam-webster.com/dictionary/culture.

"Curriculum and Resources: Charles Martel." Heritage History - Products. Accessed September 28, 2020. https://www.heritage-history.com/index.php?c=resources&s=char-dir&f=martel.

"D. Elton Trueblood." Quotes.net. Accessed September 1, 2020. https://www.quotes.net/quote/18132.

Dave's Killer Bread. "About Us." Accessed September 2, 2020. http://www.daveskillerbread.com/about-us#about-us-1.

Dave's Killer Bread. "Second Chances." Accessed September 2, 2020. http://www.daveskillerbread.com/secondchances.

"Decatur Correctional Center." Illinois.gov. Accessed August 6, 2020. https://www2.illinois.gov/idoc/facilities/Pages/decaturcorrectionalcenter.aspx.

"Demographics." Merriam-Webster.com. Accessed September 28, 2020. https://www.merriam-webster.com/dictionary/demographics.

"Dictionary by Merriam-Webster: America's Most-Trusted Online Dictionary." Merriam-Webster. Merriam-Webster. Accessed July 26, 2020. https://www.merriam-webster.com/.

"Disaster Relief & Global Health Organization." Americares. Accessed August 2, 2020. https://www.americares.org/.

Do One Thing for a Better World. Doonething.org. Project of The Emily Fund. Accessed September 2, 2020. http://www.doonething.org/.

Do One Thing for a Better World. "James Bell." Doonething.org. Accessed September 2, 2020. http://www.doonething.org/heroes/pages-b/bell-bio.htm.

Dockterman, Eliana. "Read Taylor Swift's TIME Person of the Year Interview 2017." Time. December 6, 2017. https://time.com/5049659/taylor-swift-interview-person-of-the-year-2017/.

Doctrine and Covenants 82:3. Published by The Church of Jesus Christ of Latter-day Saints, Salt Lake City, Utah. Accessed September 2, 2020. https://www.churchofjesuschrist.org/study/scriptures/dc-testament/dc/82?lang=eng.

Doyle White, Ethan. 2016. *Wicca: History, Belief, and Community in Modern Pagan Witchcraft.* Brighton: Sussex Academic Press.

Durkheim, Émile, 2008 (original observation ab. 1912). *The Elementary Forms of Religious Life,* trans. Carol Cosman and Mark S. Cladis. Oxford, UK: University of Oxford Press.

"Economic." Merriam-Webster.com. Accessed September 28, 2020. https://www.merriam-webster.com/dictionary/economic.

The Editors of Encyclopaedia Britannica. "Harriet Tubman." Encyclopedia Britannica. Encyclopedia Britannica, Inc., March 21, 2020. https://www.britannica.com/biography/Harriet-Tubman.

Edmonds, Ennis B. 2012. *Rastafari: A Very Short Introduction.* Oxford: Oxford University Press.

"Educational Equality for Ethiopian Girls." Dignity Period. Accessed August 3, 2020. https://www.dignityperiod.org/.

Elgenaidi, Maha. "Reclaiming the Sacred: Five Uniting Religious Principles." HuffPost. HuffPost, August 31, 2014. https://www.huffpost.com/entry/new_2_b_5538655?guccounter=1.

The Emily Fund for a Better World. Accessed September 2, 2020. http://www.emilyfund.org/.

Eschner, Kat. "Three Things to Know About Radical Prohibitionist Carry A. Nation." Smithsonian.com. Smithsonian Institution, December 27, 2017. https://www.smithsonianmag.com/smart-news/three-things-know-about-radical-prohibitionist-carry-nation-180967627/.

"Fair Chance Employers: Second Chance Hiring is a Win Win." GoodHire, March 11, 2020. https://www.goodhire.com/blog/fair-chance-hiring-is-a-win-win/.

Fait, Stefano. Civil Religion. Accessed August 13, 2020. https://www.mtsu.edu/first-amendment/article/1519/civil-religion.

"Faith." Dictionary.com. Accessed September 1, 2020. https://www.dictionary.com/browse/faith?s=t.

"Faith." Merriam-Webster.com. Accessed September 1, 2020. https://www.merriam-webster.com/dictionary/faith.

"Faith." The Urban Dictionary. Accessed September 1, 2020. https://www.urbandictionary.com/define.php?term=Faith.

"Faith." Vocabulary.com. Accessed September 1, 2020. https://www.vocabulary.com/dictionary/faith.

Forbes Quotes. Accessed August 23, 2020. https://www.forbes.com/quotes/author/edward-everett-hale/.

Freeman, Huey and Mark Tupper. 2014. *Legendary Locals of Decatur*. Arcadia Publishing.

Freeman, Huey. "Decatur Prison Looking for Person to Run Dog Grooming Program," July 14, 2009. Herald & Review. https://herald-review.com/news/local/decatur-prison-looking-for-person-to-run-dog-grooming-program/article_35bce2f2-7bca-5edd-aac1-ea50a4d8db84.html.

Freeman, Huey. "Pet Class Is Grooming Success in Decatur Women's Prison," February 27, 2013. Herald & Review. https://herald-review.com/news/local/pet-class-is-grooming-success-in-decatur-womens-prison/article_bb20e982-8099-11e2-8705-001a4bcf887a.html.

"Gamers Outreach: Helping Others Level up. Video Game Charity for Kids." Gamers Outreach Foundation. Accessed August 3, 2020. https://gamersoutreach.org/.

Gandhi. Film. 1982. Attenborough, Richard, Director and Producer.

Gardella, Peter. *American Civil Religion: What Americans Hold Sacred*. Oxford: University Press, 2014.

"Genesis 1: 26-28." *Common English Bible*. Nashville: Common English Bible, 2011.

"Genesis 1: 26-28." *Message Bible: Today's New International Version*. Zondervan, 2007.

"Genesis 1: 26-28." *NLT Bible: New Living Translation*. Wellington, NZ: Bible Society New Zealand, 2018.

"Genesis 1: 26-28." *Wycliffe*. Sydney: Smith, 1913.

"Genesis 12-25." *The Bible: New International Version*. London: NIV, 2008.

"George Washington." George Washington's Mount Vernon. Accessed July 30, 2020. https://www.mountvernon.org/george-washington/.

"George Washington." The White House. The United States Government. Accessed July 30, 2020. https://www.whitehouse.gov/about-the-white-house/presidents/george-washington/.

Giddens, Anthony et al. *Essentials of Sociology*, 6th Edition. W. W. Norton & Company, Inc. 2017.

Gilmore, Mikal. "The Life and Times of Bob Marley." *Rolling Stone*. Rolling Stone, February 6, 2020. https://www.rollingstone.com/music/music-news/the-life-and-times-of-bob-marley-78392/.

Global Giving Team. "A Quote to Share Every Waking Hour of World Refugee Day." Globalgiving.org. Accessed September 2, 2020. https://www.globalgiving.org/learn/12-shareable-world-refugee-day-quotes/.

"Global Nonviolent Action Database." Accessed August 2, 2020. https://nvdatabase.swarthmore.edu/category/wave-campaigns/anti-nuclear-power-movement-1960s-1980s.

"Goodwill Industries International, Inc." Goodwill Industries International. Accessed August 2, 2020. http://www.goodwill.org/.

Gorski, Philip. *American Covenant: A History of Civil Religion from the Puritans to the Present*. Princeton, NJ: Princeton University Press, 2019.

"Government." Merriam-Webster.com. Accessed September 28, 2020. https://www.merriam-webster.com/dictionary/government.

Groff, Linda, with Paul Smoker. 1996. "Spirituality, Religion, Culture, and Peace: Exploring the Foundations for Inner-Outer Peace in the 21st Century." *International Journal of Peace Studies*, vol. 1, no. 1. Accessed September 2, 2020. https://www.gmu.edu/programs/icar/ijps/vol1_1/smoker.html.

Guest, Matthew. 2011. "The Reproduction and Transmission of Religion," *The Oxford Handbook of the Sociology of Religion*, ed. Peter Clarke. Oxford, UK: University of Oxford Press.

Gupta, Dr. Sanjay. "Bill Gates' Newest Mission: Curing Alzheimer's." CNN Cable News Network. November 14, 2017. https://www.cnn.com/2017/11/13/health/bill-gates-announcement-alzheimers/index.html.

Hackett, Conrad, with David McClendon. 2017 (largely citing 2015 statistics). "Christians Remain Largest Religious Group in World, But They Are Declining in Europe." *Pew Research Center: Religion and Public Life*. Accessed September 1, 2020. https://www.pewresearch.org/fact-tank/2017/04/05/christians-remain-worlds-largest-religious-group-but-they-are-declining-in-europe/.

HarperCollins Speakers Bureau. "Nadia Hashimi: Afghan American Author and Physician." Accessed September 2, 2020. https://www.harpercollinsspeakersbureau.com/speaker/nadia-hashimi/.

Harriet Beecher Stowe Center. Accessed July 30, 2020. https://www.harrietbeecherstowecenter.org/.

Harvey, Kyle. *American Anti-Nuclear Activism, 1975-1990: The Challenge of Peace. Basingstoke: Palgrave Macmillan, 2014.*

"Healthier Lives Worldwide." *CMMB*, July 29, 2020. https://cmmb.org/.

"Helen Keller Biography." Biography | American Foundation for the Blind. Accessed July 30, 2020. https://www.afb.org/about-afb/history/helen-keller/biography-and-chronology/biography.

"Helen Keller's Life and Legacy." Helen Keller International. Accessed July 30, 2020. https://www.hki.org/helen-kellers-life-and-legacy/.

Hessler, Peter. 2017. "Meet King Akhenaten: Egypt's First Revolutionary." National Geographic. Accessed September 28, 2020. https://www.nationalgeographic.com/magazine/2017/05/akhenaten-revolutionary-egypt-king/.

History.com Editors. "Andrew Carnegie." A&E Television Networks, November 9, 2009. https://www.history.com/topics/19th-century/andrew-carnegie.

History.com Editors. "Berlin Wall." A&E Television Networks, December 15, 2009. https://www.history.com/topics/cold-war/berlin-wall.

History.com Editors. "Gay Rights." A&E Television Networks, June 28, 2017. https://www.history.com/topics/gay-rights/history-of-gay-rights.

History.com Editors. "The Holocaust." A&E Television Networks, October 14, 2009. https://www.history.com/topics/world-war-ii/the-holocaust.

History.com Editors. "'I Have a Dream' Speech." History.com. A&E Television Networks, November 30, 2017. https://www.history.com/topics/i-have-a-dream-speech.

History.com Editors. "Roe v. Wade." A&E Television Networks, March 27, 2018. https://www.history.com/topics/womens-rights/roe-v-wade.

"History - Historic Figures: Martin Luther (1483-1546)." BBC. BBC. Accessed July 31, 2020. http://www.bbc.co.uk/history/historic_figures/luther_martin.shtml.

"History of the Women's Rights Movement." National Women's History Alliance, November 5, 2019. https://nationalwomenshistoryalliance.org/history-of-the-womens-rights-movement/.

"History: The Holocaust: Home." LibGuides. Accessed July 26, 2020. https://guides.lib.jjay.cuny.edu/c.php?g=288386.

"History - William Wilberforce." BBC. BBC. Accessed August 2, 2020. http://www.bbc.co.uk/history/historic_figures/wilberforce_william.shtml.

The Holy Bible: New International Version. Grand Rapids, MI: Zondervan, 2019.

The Holy Bible: New King James Version. Nashville, TN: Thomas Nelson. 1982.

"Homer – Ancient Greek Poet – Works, Poems & Facts." Ancient Literature, April 24, 2020. https://www.ancient-literature.com/greece_homer.html.

"Hope for Humanity." Zaman International | Hope for Humanity. Accessed August 3, 2020. https://www.zamaninternational.org/.

"Hunger in America Is Growing." Feeding America. Accessed August 2, 2020. http://www.feedingamerica.org/hunger-in-america.

Hunt, Elgin F. and David C. Colander. *Social Science: An Introduction to the Study of Society*, 14th Edition. Allyn & Bacon. 2011.

"Hymn: Amazing Grace." hymnalnet RSS. Accessed July 31, 2020. https://www.hymnal.net/en/hymn/h/313.

"Ice Bucket Challenge Dramatically Accelerated the Fight against ALS." The ALS Association, June 4, 2019. https://www.als.org/stories-news/ice-bucket-challenge-dramatically-accelerated-fight-against-als.

"The Iconic Think Different Apple Commercial Narrated by Steve Jobs." Farnam Street, January 18, 2017. https://fs.blog/2016/03/steve-jobs-crazy-ones/.

"Imagine, A Center for Coping with Loss." Accessed August 3, 2020. https://www.imaginenj.org/.

"Immigrants' Rights." American Civil Liberties Union. Accessed August 3, 2020. https://www.aclu.org/issues/immigrants-rights.

"Indigenous Peoples Movement." Accessed August 3, 2020. https://indigenouspeoplesmovement.com/.

"Innovation." Merriam-Webster.com. Accessed September 28, 2020. https://www.merriam-webster.com/dictionary/innovation.

"Institution." Merriam-Webster.com. Accessed September 28, 2020. https://www.merriam-webster.com/dictionary/institution.

The Interfaith Network for the United Kingdom. Undated. "Connect: Different Faiths, Shared Values." Slideshow presentation. Accessed September 2, 2020. https://www.interfaithweek.org/uploads/connect-web.pdf.

International Christian Aid. Accessed September 2, 2020. http://www.icaid.org/.

"Isaiah 52:7" and "Isaiah 61:1-2." *Holy Bible: New International Version*. Grand Rapids, MI: Zondervan, 2019.

Islamic Relief Worldwide. Accessed September 2, 2020. https://www.islamic-relief.org/.

"Islamic Teachings: Facts about the Muslims & the Religion of Islam." May 19, 2020. https://www.whyislam.org/category/islamicteachings/.

"'I've Been to the Mountaintop' by Dr. Martin Luther King, Jr." AFSCME. Accessed August 19, 2020. https://www.afscme.org/about/history/mlk/mountaintop.

Jackson, Clay. "Decatur Prison's Grooming Program Pampers Pets Helps Rebuild Lives, " April 1, 2019. Herald & Review. https://herald-review.com/lifestyles/pets/decatur-prisons-grooming-program-pampers-pets-helps-rebuild-lives/article_95a6573d-ecab-593e-b87f-86e77523c8bf.html.

Jackson, Clay. "Grooming Groomers: Here's How Decatur Prison Grooming Program Pampers Pets, Helps Rebuild Lives," March 24, 2019. Herald & Review. https://herald-review.com/news/local/heres-how-decatur-prisons-grooming-program-pampers-pets-helps-rebuild-lives/article_29831ac1-e51d-52e8-b858-37761ec853b7.html.

Jain Pratikraman Sutras. 2014. JAINA Education Series. Raleigh, NC: Federation of Jain Associations in North America. Accessed September 2, 2020. https://jainelibrary.org/elib_master/jaina_edu/jaina_edu_book/$jes941_pratikraman_sutra_book_in_english_000249_data.pdf.

Janzen, John M. 2017. "African Religion and Healing in the Atlantic Diaspora." *Oxford Research Encyclopedias: African History*. https://oxfordre.com/africanhistory/view/10.1093/acrefore/9780190277734.001.0001/acrefore-9780190277734-e-54.

Jarus, Owen. "Alexander the Great: Facts, Biography & Accomplishments." LiveScience. Purch, August 31, 2017. https://www.livescience.com/39997-alexander-the-great.html.

Jarus, Owen. "Genghis Khan, Founder of Mongol Empire: Facts & Biography." LiveScience. Purch, February 11, 2014. https://www.livescience.com/43260-genghis-khan.html.

Jehovah's Witnesses Official Site. "How Many Jehovah's Witnesses Are There?" Accessed September 2, 2020. https://www.jw.org/en/jehovahs-witnesses/faq/how-many-jw/.

"Jimmy Carter." Accessed August 3, 2020. https://www.cartercenter.org/about/experts/jimmy_carter.html.

"Joan of Arc." Biography.com. A&E Networks Television, March 4, 2020. https://www.biography.com/military-figure/joan-of-arc.

Joan of Arc, directed by Russell Holt. 2015: Provo, UT: Go Films and BYU Broadcasting. https://www.byutv.org/show/8e53e768-8430-4b15-85fa-dee52adf9b6b/joan-of-arc?cid=ar%3Abfnt%3Ajas1%3Acontentpiece.

"Johann Sebastian Bach: A Detailed Informative Biography." Accessed July 31, 2020. http://www.baroquemusic.org/biojsbach.html.

"John Adams." The White House. The United States Government. Accessed July 31, 2020. https://www.whitehouse.gov/about-the-white-house/presidents/john-adams/.

"John Calvin." Calvin University. Accessed July 31, 2020. https://calvin.edu/about/history/john-calvin.html.

"John Greenleaf Whittier." Poets.org. Accessed September 2, 2020. https://poets.org/poet/john-greenleaf-whittier.

Johnson, Todd M., and Brian J. Grim. 2013. *The World's Religions in Figures: An Introduction to International Religious Demography*. Malden, MA: John Wiley and Sons.

Johnstone, Ronald L. 2006. Religion in Society: A Sociology of Religion. 8th ed. Upper Saddle River, NJ: Pearson/Prentice-Hall.

Juan, Stephen. "What are the Most Widely Practiced Religions in the World?" The Register. Accessed September 1, 2020. https://www.theregister.com/2006/10/06/the_odd_body_religion/.

"Julius Caesar." Shakespeare Birthplace Trust. Accessed July 31, 2020. https://www.shakespeare.org.uk/explore-shakespeare/shakespedia/shakespeares-plays/julius-caesar/.

JustServe. Sponsored by The Church of Jesus Christ of Latter-day Saints. Accessed September 2, 2020. https://www.justserve.org/.

Keller, Helen. *My Religion*. Literary Licensing, 2011.

Kemerling, Garth. "Plato." Accessed August 1, 2020. http://www.philosophypages.com/ph/plat.htm.

Kemerling, Garth. "Socrates." Accessed August 2, 2020. http://www.philosophypages.com/ph/socr.htm.

Kendall, Diana. *Sociology in Our Times*, 8th Edition. Wadsworth Cengage Learning, 2011.

Keneally, Thomas, and Sam J. Lundwall. *Schindlers Ark*. Stockholm: Norstedt, 1983.

The King Center. July 28, 2020. http://www.thekingcenter.org/.

King Jr., Martin Luther. *Draft of Dr. Martin Luther King Jr Address: March on Washington for Jobs and Freedom, Lincoln Memorial*. August 28, 1963.

King Jr., Martin Luther. August 28, 1963. "I Have a Dream." Address delivered at the March on Washington for Jobs and Freedom. The Martin Luther King Jr. Research and Education Institute, Stanford University. Accessed September 2, 2020. https://kinginstitute.stanford.edu/king-papers/documents/i-have-dream-address-delivered-march-washington-jobs-and-freedom.

Kiprop, Joseph. September 19, 2017. "Top Countries in the World by Zoroastrian Population." WorldAtlas.com. Accessed September 2, 2020. https://www.worldatlas.com/articles/top-countries-of-the-world-by-zoroastrian-population.html.

Klingenberg, Maria, with Sofia Sjö. 2019. "Theorizing Religious Socialization: A Critical Assessment." *Religion*, vol. 49 no. 2, pp. 163-178. https://doi.org/10.1080/0048721X.2019.1584349.

Küng, Hans. 2004. *Global Responsibility: In Search of a New World Ethic*. Eugene, OR: Wipf and Stock Publishers.

"Lakota Chief Biographies." Akta Lakota Museum & Cultural Center. Accessed August 1, 2020. http://aktalakota.stjo.org/site/PageServer?pagename=alm_culture_chief_bios.

"Lao Tzu-." The School of Life Articles, March 31, 2015. https://www.theschooloflife.com/thebookoflife/the-great-eastern-philosophers-lao-tzu/.

Laozi, and James Legge. *Tao Te Ching*. Mineola: Ixia Press, 2020.

"The Largest Immigrant Youth-Led Network in the Country," March 22, 2020. https://unitedwedream.org/.

Law, Bill. "Razed Mosque Symbol of Divided Bahrain." BBC News. BBC, March 27, 2014. https://www.bbc.com/news/world-middle-east-26721084.

Lee, Spike and Arnold Perl. *Malcolm X*, Film. 1992.

"The Leonardo DiCaprio Foundation." Accessed August 3, 2020. https://www.leonardodicaprio.org/.

Levin, Paul T. *Turkey and the European Union: Christian and Secular Images of Islam.* Palgrave Macmillian. 2011.

Levy, Darlene. Dec. 3, 2012. "Helping Those in Need around the Holidays." Purdue Global University. Accessed September 2, 2020 https://www.purdueglobal.edu/blog/social-behavioral-sciences/helping-those-in-need/.

"The Life of Baha'u'llah." The Life of Bahá'u'lláh. Accessed July 29, 2020. https://www.bahaullah.org/.

"The Life of Oliver Cromwell." Historic UK. Accessed August 1, 2020. https://www.historic-uk.com/HistoryUK/HistoryofEngland/Oliver-Cromwell/.

Lipka, Michael. March 8, 2016. "Unlike US, Few Jews in Israel Identify as Reform or Conservative." *Pew Research Center: Religion and Public Life.* Accessed September 2, 2020. https://www.pewresearch.org/fact-tank/2016/03/15/unlike-u-s-few-jews-in-israel-identify-as-reform-or-conservative/.

"Luke 10:25-28." *Holy Bible: New International Version.* Grand Rapids, MI: Zondervan, 2019.

Luther, Martin, and Kurt Aland. *Martin Luther's 95 Theses: with the Pertinent Documents from the History of the Reformation.* Saint Louis, MO: Concordia Pub House, 2004.

Macionis, John J. *Sociology*, 15th Edition. Pearson. 2014.

"Mahatma Gandhi." Biography.com. A&E Networks Television, September 4, 2019. https://www.biography.com/people/mahatma-gandhi-9305898.

"Mahatma Gandhi." Sky HISTORY. Accessed August 3, 2020. http://www.history.co.uk/biographies/mahatma-gandhi.

Mandela, Nelson. *Address to the Zionist Christian Church's Easter Conferences.* 1994.

"MAP International Home - Medicine for the World." Accessed August 2, 2020. https://www.map.org/.

"March For Our Lives." June 19, 2020. https://marchforourlives.com/mission-story/.

"March on Washington for Jobs and Freedom." The Martin Luther King, Jr., Research and Education Institute, May 30, 2019. https://kinginstitute.stanford.edu/encyclopedia/march-washington-jobs-and-freedom.

"Margaret Mead Quotes." BrainyQuote. Xplore. Accessed July 26, 2020. https://www.brainyquote.com/quotes/margaret_mead_100502.

"Mark 12:28-31." *Holy Bible: New International Version.* Grand Rapids, MI: Zondervan, 2019.

Mark, Joshua J. "Charlemagne." Ancient History Encyclopedia. Ancient History Encyclopedia, July 25, 2020. https://www.ancient.eu/Charlemagne/.

Marx, Karl, Algernon Lee, and Friedrich Engels. 1946. *Essentials of Marx: The Communist Manifesto.* New York: Rand School Press, 1946 (original observation ab. 1848).

Marx, Karl. *"Marx, A Contribution to the Critique of Hegel's Philosophy of Right 1844."* Accessed July 29, 2020. https://www.marxists.org/archive/marx/works/1843/critique-hpr/intro.htm.

Massey, Garth. *Ways of Social Change: Making Sense of Modern Times.* 2nd Edition. Sage Publications, Inc., 2016.

"Matthew 22: 35-40." *Holy Bible: New International Version.* Grand Rapids, MI: Zondervan, 2019.

Maybee, Julie E., 2019. "Hegel's Dialectics." *The Stanford Encyclopedia of Philosophy* (Winter 2019 Edition), Edward N. Zalta (ed.). https://plato.stanford.edu/archives/win2019/entries/hegel-dialectics/.

McEvers, Kelly. "Bahrain: The Revolution That Wasn't." NPR. NPR, January 5, 2012. https://www.npr.org/2012/01/05/144637499/bahrain-the-revolution-that-wasnt.

Metmuseum.org. Accessed July 31, 2020. https://www.metmuseum.org/toah/hd/just/hd_just.htm.

Metmuseum.org. Accessed July 31, 2020. https://www.metmuseum.org/toah/hd/suly/hd_suly.htm.

"Me Too. Movement." July 17, 2020. https://metoomvmt.org/.

"Micah 6:8." *Holy Bible: New International Version.* Grand Rapids, MI: Zondervan, 2019.

"Michelangelo, His Paintings, and Sculptures." Accessed August 1, 2020. https://www.michelangelo.org/.

"Michigan Legislature." Accessed August 13, 2020. http://www.legislature.mi.gov/(S(pknfcq2oj4b5apgskbjtgfqc))/mileg.aspx?page=getObject.

Miles of Freedom site. Accessed September 2, 2020. http://milesoffreedom.org/.

The Miracle Worker. Film. Playfilm Productions. 1962.

Missouri Secretary of State - IT. "The Missouri Mormon War." Missouri State Seal. Accessed August 13, 2020. https://www.sos.mo.gov/archives/resources/findingaids/miscMormonRecords/eo.

"Mothers Against Drunk Driving." MADD. Accessed August 3, 2020. https://www.madd.org/.

"Mother Teresa of Calcutta." Accessed August 3, 2020. http://www.motherteresa.org/.

Moving Arts Española. Accessed August 3, 2020. https://www.movingartsespanola.org/.

"NAACP." Accessed August 2, 2020. https://www.naacp.org/.

The Napoleon Series, April 4, 2020. https://www.napoleon-series.org/.

National Immigration Law Center, April 24, 2020. https://www.nilc.org/.

"The Nation's Oldest & Largest Pro-Life Organization." National Right to Life. Accessed July 26, 2020. https://www.nrlc.org/.

Nature News. Nature Publishing Group. Accessed July 30, 2020. https://www.nature.com/scitable/topicpage/gregor-mendel-a-private-scientist-6618227/.

"NDGAA." National Dog Groomers Association of America. Accessed August 6, 2020. https://nationaldoggroomers.com/.

Newman, David M. *Sociology: Exploring the Architecture of Everyday Life*, Brief Edition. Sage, 2011.

"New on ADA.gov." ADA.gov homepage. Accessed August 3, 2020. https://www.ada.gov/.

Nicholls, Walter J. *The Immigrant Rights Movement: The Battle Over National Citizenship*. Stanford: Stanford University Press. 2019.

Nijssen, Daan. "Cyrus the Great." Ancient History Encyclopedia. Ancient History Encyclopedia, July 22, 2020. https://www.ancient.eu/Cyrus_the_Great/.

"Noah's Animal House." Accessed August 3, 2020. https://noahsanimalhouse.org/.

"NRDC – Natural Resources Defense Council." Accessed August 2, 2020. https://www.nrdc.org/.

Nye, Catrin, and Joshua Baker. "The Calais Conversation That Left Lily Allen in Tears." BBC News. BBC, October 12, 2016. https://www.bbc.com/news/entertainment-arts-37607774.

"The Obama Presidential Center and the Obama Foundation." Accessed July 26, 2020. https://www.obama.org/.

The Office of Barack and Michelle Obama. Accessed July 26, 2020. https://barackobama.com/about/.

"Oskar Schindler." Accessed August 1, 2020. https://www.jewishvirtuallibrary.org/oskar-schindler.

Otto, Rudolf. 1923. *The Idea of the Holy*. Trans. John W. Harvey. Oxford: Oxford University Press.

Ottoman. Accessed August 2, 2020. http://www.theottomans.org/english/family/suleyman1.asp.

"Our Labor History, Timeline: AFL-CIO." AFL. Accessed August 3, 2020. https://aflcio.org/about-us/history.

"Our Programs." The Task Force for Global Health. Accessed September 28, 2020. https://taskforce.org/our-programs/.

"Our Rescue." Peaceful Valley Donkey Rescue. Accessed August 3, 2020. https://donkeyrescue.org/our-rescue/.

Perez Jr., Juan and Monique Garcia. "Chance the Rapper Writes $1 Million Check to CPS as a 'Call to Action.'" chicagotribune.com, March 7, 2017. https://www.chicagotribune.com/politics/ct-chance-the-rapper-chicago-schools-plan-met-20170306-story.html.

"Petition for Woman Suffrage." US House of Representatives: History, Art & Archives. Accessed July 26, 2020. https://history.house.gov/Records-and-Research/Listing/pm_012/.

Pew Research Center Staff, Dec. 19, 2011. "Christian Traditions." *Pew Research Center: Religion and Public Life. Accessed September 2, 2020.* https://www.pewforum.org/2011/12/19/global-christianity-traditions/#protestant.

Pew Research Center Staff, Dec. 18, 2012. "The Global Religious Landscape: Buddhists." *Pew Research Center: Religion and Public Life. Accessed September 2, 2020.* https://www.pewforum.org/2012/12/18/global-religious-landscape-buddhist/.

Pew Research Center Staff, Dec. 18, 2012. "The Global Religious Landscape: Folk Religionists." *Pew Research Center: Religion and Public Life. Accessed September 2, 2020.* https://www.pewforum.org/2012/12/18/global-religious-landscape-folk/.

Pew Research Center Staff, Dec. 18, 2012. "The Global Religious Landscape: Hindus." *Pew Research Center: Religion and Public Life. Accessed September 2, 2020.* https://www.pewforum.org/2012/12/18/global-religious-landscape-hindu/.

Pew Research Center Staff, April 2, 2015. "Jews." (Subsection of "The Future of World Religions: Population Growth Projections, 2010-2050.") *Pew Research Center: Religion and Public Life. Accessed September 2, 2020.* https://www.pewforum.org/2015/04/02/jews/.

Pew Research Center Staff, April 2, 2015. "Other Religions." (Subsection of "The Future of World Religions: Population Growth Projections, 2010-2050.") *Pew Research Center: Religion and Public Life. Accessed September 2, 2020.* https://www.pewforum.org/2015/04/02/other-religions/.

Pew Research Center Staff, April 2, 2015. "The Future of World Religions: Population Growth Projections, 2010-2050." *Pew Research Center: Religion and Public Life. Accessed September 2, 2020.* https://www.pewforum.org/2015/04/02/religious-projections-2010-2050/.

Pew Research Center Staff, Apr. 5, 2017. "The Changing Global Religious Landscape." *Pew Research Center: Religion and Public Life. Accessed September 2, 2020.* https://www.pewforum.org/2017/04/05/the-changing-global-religious-landscape/.

Pew Research Center Staff, Nov. 8, 2017. "Orthodox Christianity in the 21st Century." *Pew Research Center: Religion and Public Life. Accessed September 2, 2020.* https://www.pewforum.org/2017/11/08/orthodox-christianity-in-the-21st-century/.

"Political." Merriam-Webster.com. Accessed September 28, 2020. https://www.merriam-webster.com/dictionary/political.

Posner, Sarah. Nov. 19, 2012. "Kosher Jesus: Messianic Jews in the Holy Land." *The Atlantic. Accessed September 2, 2020.* https://www.theatlantic.com/international/archive/2012/11/kosher-jesus-messianic-jews-in-the-holy-land/265670/.

"Pray with Us." Food For The Poor | Feeding the Hungry | Charity organization, August 13, 2020. http://www.foodforthepoor.org/.

"Proposition 35. Human Trafficking. Penalties. Initiative Statue." California Secretary of State. Accessed July 26, 2020. https://vig.cdn.sos.ca.gov/2012/general/pdf/35-title-summ-analysis.pdf.

"Rabindranath Tagore Quotes." BrainyQuote. Accessed September 1, 2020. https://www.brainyquote.com/quotes/rabindranath_tagore_121379.

Rattini, Kristin Baird. "Who Was Augustus Caesar?" Augustus Caesar-facts and information, May 20, 2019. https://www.nationalgeographic.com/culture/people/reference/augustus-caesar/.

Rauschenbusch, Walter. *Christianity and the Social Crisis.* New York: MacMillan, 1907.

Rauschenbusch, Walter. *Christianizing the Social Order.* The classics Us (republication), 2013.

Rauschenbusch, Walter. *Social Principles of Jesus.* BIBLIOTECH Press (republication), 2020.

Redd, Nola Taylor. "Galileo Galilei: Biography, Inventions & Other Facts." Space.com. Space, November 14, 2017. https://www.space.com/15589-galileo-galilei.html.

Redd, Nola Taylor. "Nicolaus Copernicus Biography: Facts & Discoveries." Space.com. Space, March 20, 2018. https://www.space.com/15684-nicolaus-copernicus.html.

"Reducing Poverty in America." Catholic Charities USA, July 29, 2020. https://www.catholiccharitiesusa.org/.

"Relief Done Right." Direct Relief. Direct Relief, June 18, 2020. https://www.directrelief.org/.

Reynolds, Barbara A. (ed.), 1988. *And Still We Rise: Interviews With 50 Black Role Models.* Washington D.C.: USA Today Books (Gannett), pp. 73-75.

Rhodan, Maya. "Barack Obama: Read His First Remarks Since Leaving Office." Time. Time, April 24, 2017. https://time.com/4753027/barack-obama-university-of-chicago-speech-transcript/.

Ricketts, Colin. "A Summary of Julius Caesar's Life and Achievements." History Hit. History Hit, June 7, 2019. https://www.historyhit.com/a-summary-of-julius-caesars-life-and-achievements/.

The Right Livelihood Foundation. Undated. "Anwar Fazal (1982-, Malaysia)." Accessed September 2, 2020. https://www.rightlivelihoodaward.org/laureates/anwar-fazal/.

"Rotary International." Home | Rotary International. Accessed August 2, 2020. https://www.rotary.org/.

Rothman, Emily. April 28, 2015. "What Martin Luther King Jr Really Thought about Riots." Time. Accessed September 17, 2020. https://time.com/3838515/baltimore-riots-language-unheard-quote/.

"RV4CampfireFamily." Accessed August 3, 2020. https://rv4campfirefamily.org/.

"The Salvation Army USA." Accessed August 2, 2020. https://www.salvationarmyusa.org/usn/.

"Samaritan's Purse Home Page." Samaritan's Purse. Accessed August 2, 2020. https://www.samaritanspurse.org/.

Sangrula, Sakchham. June 20, 2019. "What are the Basic Beliefs of the Tenrikyo Religion?" Worldatlas.com. Accessed September 2, 2020. https://www.worldatlas.com/articles/what-is-tenriism-tenrikyo.html.

Schindler's List. Film. Universal Studios. 1993.

Scott, Donald. "The Religious Origins of Manifest Destiny." *Divining America. TeacherServe, National Humanities Center. Accessed August 2, 2020.* http://nationalhumanitiescenter.org/tserve/nineteen/nkeyinfo/mandestiny.htm.

"Section 36A." General Law - Part IV, Title I, Chapter 272, Section 36A. Accessed August 13, 2020. https://malegislature.gov/Laws/GeneralLaws/PartIV/TitleI/Chapter272/Section36a.

"Serving Families and Individuals in the Greater Boston Area." Lend a Hand Society. Accessed August 23, 2020. http://www.lend-a-hand-society.org/.

"Sexual and Reproductive Rights." Sexual and Reproductive Rights | Amnesty International. Accessed August 3, 2020. https://www.amnesty.org/en/what-we-do/sexual-and-reproductive-rights/.

Sherkat, Darren. 2003. "Religious Socialization." *Handbook of the Sociology of Religion*, ed. Michele Dillon. Cambridge, UK: Cambridge University Press. https://www.cambridge.org/core/books/handbook-of-the-sociology-of-religion/religious-socialization/015E3C47D5548A69A25155F242506D3D.

"Sikh Aid: Global Disaster Relief." United Sikhs. Accessed September 2, 2020. https://unitedsikhs.org/disaster-relief-sikh-aid/.

Skeet, Ann, with Patrick Coutermarsh. June 1, 2015. "In Search of a Global Ethic." Markkula Center for Applied Ethics at Santa Clara University. Accessed September 2, 2020. https://www.scu.edu/ethics/focus-areas/business-ethics/resources/in-search-of-a-global-ethic/.

"Social Change Sayings and Quotes." Accessed August 19, 2020. https://www.wiseoldsayings.com/social-change-quotes/#ixzz6U7XSz9ju.

"Spain – The Golden Age - Ferdinand and Isabella." Accessed July 31, 2020. http://countrystudies.us/spain/7.htm.

St. Jude Children's Research Hospital. Accessed August 2, 2020. https://www.stjude.org/.

Staff, NPR. "The Arab Spring: A Year of Revolution," December 17, 2011. https://www.npr.org/2011/12/17/143897126/the-arab-spring-a-year-of-revolution.

Stulberg, Lisa M. *LGBTQ Social Movements*. Cambridge: Polity, 2018.

Swatos, William. "Church-Sect Theory." Hartford Institute for Religion. Research. Accessed August 13, 2020. http://hirr.hartsem.edu/ency/cstheory.htm.

Tafreshi, Photograph by Babak. "Cyrus the Great: History's Most Merciful Conqueror?" National Geographic, May 27, 2020. https://www.nationalgeographic.com/culture/people/reference/cyrus-the-great/.

"Take the First Step in Faith." … Quote Investigator. Accessed September 1, 2020. https://quoteinvestigator.com/2019/04/18/staircase/#note-135686-5R.

"Taking on Big Problems and Making Real Impact." The Task Force for Global Health, July 28, 2020. https://www.taskforce.org/.

Tallon, Mark. "CLIP Program Gives Prison Inmates, Shelter Pets Chance at Fresh Start'" November 30, 2006. Herald & Review. https://herald-review.com/news/local/clip-program-gives-prison-inmates-shelter-pets-chance-at-fresh-start/article_f314395a-a14d-5b5d-bc8c-cd0c9fbd9cb2.html.

Taronas, Laura. Harvard University. "Akhenaten: The Mysteries of Religious Revolution." ARCE. Accessed August 1, 2020. https://www.arce.org/resource/akhenaten-mysteries-religious-revolution.

Their Story is Our Story: Giving Voice to Refugees. Accessed September 2, 2020.
https://tsosrefugees.org/.

Theodorou, Angelina. "5 Facts about Israeli Druze, a Unique Religious and Ethnic Group."
Pew Research Center: Religion and Public Life. Accessed September 2, 2020.
https://www.pewresearch.org/fact-tank/2016/03/21/5-facts-about-israeli-druze-
a-unique-religious-and-ethnic-group/.

Thompson, Dave. "Brotherhood of Man: Biography & History." Accessed August 19, 2020.
https://www.allmusic.com/artist/brotherhood-of-man-mn0000523715/biography.

"TIME'S UP Now. Join Us." Accessed August 2, 2020. https://www.timesupnow.com/.

Trump, Donald. Twitter post, December 31, 2014. http://twitter.com/realDonaldTrump.

"UFW History." UFW. Accessed August 2, 2020. https://ufw.org/research/history/ufw-history/.

Unitarian Universalist Association. 2020. "UUA Membership Statistics, 1961-2020." *Demographic
and Statistical Information about Unitarian Universalism*. Accessed September 2, 2020.
https://www.uua.org/data/demographics/uua-statistics.

"United Nations Entity for Gender Equality and the Empowerment of Women." UN Women.
Accessed August 3, 2020. https://www.unwomen.org/en.

"United Nations Foundation: Helping the UN Build a Better World." Accessed August 2, 2020.
http://www.unfoundation.org/.

United Way Worldwide. Accessed August 2, 2020. http://unitedwayworldwide.org/.

Valente, Judy. Aug. 1, 2008. "Christian Science Healing." Interview transcript for *PBS:
Religion and Ethics Newsweekly*. Accessed September 2, 2020. https://www.pbs.org/wnet/
religionandethics/2008/08/01/christian-science-healing/6/.

Violatti, Cristian. "Jesus Christ." Ancient History Encyclopedia. Ancient History Encyclopedia,
July 28, 2020. https://www.ancient.eu/Jesus_Christ/.

W. Haywood Burns Institute. Accessed September 2, 2020. https://www.burnsinstitute.org/.

"Walter Rauschenbusch." Christian History | Learn the History of Christianity & the Church.
Christian History, August 8, 2008. https://www.christianitytoday.com/history/people/
activists/walter-rauschenbusch.html.

"Watts Riots." Civil Rights Digital Library. Accessed July 26, 2020.
http://crdl.usg.edu/events/watts_riots/?Welcome.

"We Build Tools to Defend Children from Sexual Abuse." Thorn, July 22, 2020.
https://www.thorn.org/.

Weikart, Richard. *Hitler's Religion: The Twisted Beliefs That Drove the Third Reich*. Washington,
DC: Regnery History. 2016.

Weitzman, Mark. *"Antisemitism: A Historical Survey."* Accessed August 2, 2020.
http://www.museumoftolerance.com/education/teacher-resources/holocaust-resources/
antisemitism-a-historical-survey.html.

"Welcome to Give.org." Accessed August 2, 2020. http://www.give.org/.

Wessler, Nathan Freed. "The Supreme Court's Most Consequential Ruling for Privacy in the Digital Age, One Year In." American Civil Liberties Union. American Civil Liberties Union, June 28, 2019. https://www.aclu.org/blog/privacy-technology/location-tracking/supreme-courts-most-consequential-ruling-privacy-digital.

West, Cornel. 1997. Interview with Henry Louis Gates for *PBS: Frontline. Episode aired February 10, 1998. Interview transcript. Accessed September 1, 2020.* https://www.pbs.org/wgbh/pages/frontline/shows/race/interviews/west.html.

"What Does Genesis 1:26 Mean? 'Then God Said, 'Let Us Make Mankind in Our Image, in Our Likeness, so That They May Rule over the Fish in the Sea and the Birds in the Sky, over the Livesto." Bible Study Tools. Accessed August 23, 2020. https://www.biblestudytools.com/genesis/1-26-compare.html.

"What Does Genesis 1:28 Mean? 'God Blessed Them and Said to Them, 'Be Fruitful and Increase in Number; Fill the Earth and Subdue It.'"" Bible Study Tools. Accessed August 23, 2020. https://www.biblestudytools.com/genesis/1-28-compare.html.

"What Is Buddhism? The Buddhist Centre." What is Buddhism? | The Buddhist Centre. Accessed July 30, 2020. https://thebuddhistcentre.com/buddhism.

"William Wordsworth Quotes." BrainyQuote. Accessed September 1, 2020. https://www.brainyquote.com/authors/william-wordsworth-quotes.

Wilson, Christopher. "Lessons Worth Learning From the Moment Four Students Sat Down to Take a Stand." Smithsonian.com. Smithsonian Institution. Accessed July 26, 2020. https://www.smithsonianmag.com/smithsonian-institution/lessons-worth-learning-moment-greensboro-four-sat-down-lunch-counter-180974087/.

Witt, Jon. *SOC 2009*. McGraw-Hill, 2009.

"Women's Rights." Human Rights Watch. Accessed August 3, 2020. https://www.hrw.org/topic/womens-rights.

Woodley, Shailene. "Shailene Woodley: I Was Arrested Fighting Dakota Pipeline." Time. Time, October 20, 2016. https://time.com/4538557/shailene-woodley-arrest-pipeline/.

Worldometer. Undated. "North Korea Population (Live)." Accessed September 2, 2020. https://www.worldometers.info/world-population/north-korea-population/#:~:text=North%20Korea%202020%20population%20is,(and%20dependencies)%20by%20population.

"YMCA of the USA." The Y, August 1, 2020. http://www.ymca.net/.

"Your Guide To Intelligent Giving: Home." Charity Navigator. Accessed August 2, 2020. https://www.charitynavigator.org/.

Zavada, Jack. March 1, 2019. "What do Unitarian Universalists Believe?" LearnReligions.com. Accessed September 2, 2020. https://www.learnreligions.com/unitarian-universalist-beliefs-and-practices-701571.

Zax, David. "Galileo's Revolutionary Vision Helped Usher In Modern Astronomy." Smithsonian. com. Smithsonian Institution, August 1, 2009. https://www.smithsonianmag.com/science-nature/Galileos-Revolutionary-Vision-Helped-Usher-In-Modern-Astronomy-34545274/.

[Author removed at request of original publisher]. "17.3 Sociological Perspectives on Religion," April 8, 2016. https://open.lib.umn.edu/sociology/chapter/17-3-sociological-perspectives-on-religion/.

[Author removed at request of original publisher]. "Chapter 4: Socialization," September 1, 2020. https://open.lib.umn.edu/sociology/part/chapter-4-socialization/.

INDEX

I

Immigrants' Rights movement, 60
implicit religion
  concept of, 24, 36, 40, 54, 62, 77, 84, 95, 105
  significance of, 24
inculcation, procedure of, 22
Indigenous Peoples movement, 61
individuals, motivated by religious concerns, 69–75
indoctrination, procedure of, 22
Inquisition, the, 37
institutional motivation, for social change, 42
Inter Caetera (1493), 48
Interfaith Network, 34
interfaith relations, 33
International Christian Aid, 107
Islamic Relief, 107

J

Jain Pratikraman Sutra, 34
Joan of Arc, 56, 62, 72, 105–106
job skills, development of, 91
Jobs, Steve, 10–11
Johnstone, Ronald, 20
Judeo-Christian Ten Commandments, 39
Just Serve, 107

K

Kim and Correctional Ladies Improving Pets (CLIP) case study, 87–90, 91
Kimmel, Jimmy, 79
King, Martin Luther, Jr., 34, 56–57, 76, 106
Küng, Hans, 34, 94
Kushner, Ashton, 78–79

L

Labor Movement in America, 61
Leonardo DiCaprio Foundation, 79
Levy, Darlene, 34
LGBTQ Social Movement, 60

life, respect for, 35, 38, 48, 57, 84, 94, 105 .
Liz, story of, 95–98, 100

M

Mandela, Nelson, 77
MAP International, 46
March For Our Lives, 57
Mars, Bruno, 80
Martin, Trayvon, 57
Marx, Karl, 21, 53
Mebrahtu, Freweini, 81
#MeToo movement, 58
Meyers, Mark, 82
Miles of Freedom, 82
Miles, Richard, 82
Montoya, Roger, 83
Moore, Demi, 78–79
Mormon Wars of 1830s, 39
Mothers Against Drunk Drivers (MADD), 61
motivators, of social change, 9
  cultural shifts, 11
  demographic changes, 11
  economic restructuring, 12
  governmental and political activities, 12–13
  religious concerns and, 15, 90
  scientific and technological innovations, 13–14
  social-institutional shifts, 14–15
multi-racial marriages, 4
Musa, story of, 101
mysterium tremendum (1923), 20
mythological resonance, 56

N

Natural Resource Defense Council, 48
Nazi aggression, 37
needs of society, 10
neglected tropical diseases (NTDs), 43
New Religious Movements, 42
New Testament, 27, 91

Noah's Animal House, 81

non-governmental organizations (NGOs), 47, 86, 96

non-violent civil disobedience, 76

O

Obama, Barack, 67

Obamacare, 79

observations, on social change, 4

Old Testament, 56

others, respect for, 35, 39, 57, 94

Otto, Rudolf, 20

P

political, definition of, 12

political freedom, 16

poverty eradication, 47

proletariat (lower class), 21

pro-life movement. *see* Right-to-Life movement

Q

quasi-religious devotion, 40

R

racial inequality, 77

religion

billion-member religions, 28

civil religion, 40

common values, 34–35

contribution of social change, 22

examination of world's major religions, 27

hundred-million-member religions, 29

likely less than a million or population unknown, 32

likely million-member religions, 31

Marx's views on, 21

million-member religions, 30

"superpowers" of, 21

as "the opium of the people," 21

religion and conscience, freedom of, 35, 39, 57, 94, 105

religion-sponsored social events, 21

religious belief and behavior

downsides of, 21

religious concerns, 15, 39

religious conflict, 21

religious cults, 86

religious devotion, 40

religious experiences, idea of, 56, 62

religious extremist terrorism, 37

religious faith

commonalities between, 25

common values, 34–35

component of, 20

definition of, 7, 16, 19–20, 85

as group phenomenon, 20

idea of, 25

landscape of, 27

leap of faith, 22

meaning of, 27

as platform and rationale for violent social change, 37

principles of, 83

as propaganda used to solidify support for war and violence, 37

sense of, 97

religious identities, 27

religious institutions, 37

religious literacy, 33

religious mission, 33

religious motivation, for social change, 90

religious organizations, 41

religious socialization, 25, 55, 94, 104

Right-to-Life movement, 4

Robinson, Mary, 83

Roman expansion, 37

Rotary Foundation, 46

RV4CampfireFamily, 81

S

Sacks, Rabbi, 27

sacred canopy, 20

sadaqah, 34

9 781792 437571